CALLING A CITY

I dedicate this book to Mary,
my wife for over forty years,
for her tolerance towards the way this project
has eaten into our quality time.

Calling a City Back to God

PADDY MALLON

KINGSWAY PUBLICATIONS
EASTBOURNE

ISBN 1 84291 116 3

Published by
KINGSWAY COMMUNICATIONS LTD
Lottbridge Drove, Eastbourne BN23 6NT, England.
Email: books@kingsway.co.uk

Book design and production for the publishers by
Bookprint Creative Services, P.O. Box 827, BN21 3YJ, England.
Printed in Great Britain.

Contents

Preface

In Robert Warren's excellent account of his ministry at the
Sheffield church St Thomas's, *In the Crucible*, he was gracious
enough to record as the last item under 'Diary of Events' my
arrival as the Baptist minister. While this was an accurate reflection of chronological events up to that point, several of my
friends humorously suggested that my coming must therefore
be the climax of the church's history. Nothing could be further
from the truth. A Baptist minister friend of mine, who helped
me in my decision to pursue training for the ordained ministry,
confessed to the difficulty he had in coming to terms with the
fact that the kingdom of God did not depend on him – a senti-
ment I share. All who are engaged in ministry within the
church, whether in leadership or as serving members, know that
it is Jesus who builds his church and graciously uses each one
of us in the process.

I have had the privilege of being part of St Thomas's leadership team since 1988, and trying to tell the story so far of how the
church functions would be rather like taking a still photograph of

a moving drama. This is not a chronological account of developments at St Thomas's, but rather an attempt to share the principles behind what we do, with snapshots and examples from our experiences along the way. To some who read this book, the church may well give the appearance of running like a well-oiled machine. The reality is that all of us are on a journey and the landscape of the church's mission is constantly changing, sometimes requiring rapid adaptation to meet new opportunities. It is not all plain sailing, but we are blessed with a membership accustomed to change. In the economy of things, some members are able to adapt more easily than others; some assimilate and apply the vision and values of the church readily, while others struggle; some understand the dynamics of how we do church more than others; some feel the warmth and benefit of intimate fellowship, others feel they are on the edge of the church. The truth is that the church is made up of human beings, albeit redeemed, who are bound to reflect apparent weaknesses as well as strengths, and there are bound to be blind spots at leadership level as well as among the rank-and-file members. It is a sign and a wonder to me that the people of St Thomas's are so committed to the Lord of the church, and to be part of the leadership there has been a highlight of my 50 years as a Christian.

The content of this book arose out of a dissertation I submitted to Fuller Theological Seminary, Pasadena, California as part of their Doctor of Ministry programme. I am grateful to Dr Eddie Gibbs, my supervisor, for the assistance and helpful insight he gave. I thank Ruth Aidley, a member of staff at St Thomas's, who proofread the dissertation, and Elizabeth Bumpas from the USA, who acted as my personal assistant during her time at the church and helped considerably in the preparation of this book. I count it an honour to work with

Mike Breen, the leader of the team at St Thomas's, whose unwavering commitment to the integrity of the gospel and the word of God has been an inspiration.

Finally, I hope the book will provide a fresh theological and biblical approach that will help churches to realise the potential that exists within any fellowship, so that disciples may become mature in their faith, using the gifts of God's Holy Spirit. I offer my thoughts in the hope that the methods used at St Thomas's, when adapted to any local church, regardless of its tradition or denominational affiliation, can facilitate healthy growth and advancement of God's kingdom.

Foreword

Sheffield is one of the great cities of England and the birthplace of the modern steel industry. Today Sheffield and the other cities of England are like Nineveh many years ago – thousands live in close proximity but most do not 'know their right hand from their left'.

Of course, it is the church's responsibility to show these people the way, but if it were easy everyone would be doing it. The question is how? How do we reach these great urban populations with the ageless gospel in our day? This has been the question that Paddy and the other leaders of St Thomas's Church, Sheffield, have been grappling with for many years, and in this book you will find his reflections on how this has been attempted and achieved.

Serving the purposes of God by planting and growing kingdom work in such a city as Sheffield is an exciting and challenging enterprise. It forces you to think through your theology and practice at the deepest levels. It causes you to rethink what the church really is. Paddy's book gets to grips with these questions and contributes many important new elements to our thinking on mission.

The themes and scope of this book are wide and yet are deftly handled so that this highly complex task is presented in a simple and readable fashion. Paddy has, I believe, provided the church in this land and beyond with an invaluable resource that will enable us to continue to think through the obstacles and opportunities of urban mission for Jesus to come. In its pages you will find vision for a new future and equipping for the task. May the Lord answer our prayers and raise up many churches to call their cities back to God.

Mike Breen

Introduction

It has never been easy to win people to faith in Jesus Christ. Yet when Christianity burst upon the world with its good news, it was proclaimed with great enthusiasm and courage by its disciples, who, for the most part, were ordinary members of society. It is hard to miss the message that the church needs to be evangelistic in each and every generation, part of the process in which the Holy Spirit convicts people that Jesus Christ is the Lord and Saviour of all the earth. This message is increasingly urgent today. Despite the many programmes imported mainly from the USA, as well as initiatives from agencies in the UK claiming their methodology as the panacea for all previous ills, the church in the West, and in the UK especially, seems unable to achieve the same kind of effect as the early church did.

The current crisis of confidence in the Western church belies an underlying commitment to this end, and is in marked contrast to the growth and vitality of the church in the developing world. The US Center for World Mission reports an unprecedented growth of the church – except in the so-called developed world.

In Nigeria, for example, the Redeemed Christian Church of God (RCCG), led by Pastor Enoch Adeboye, is the fastest-growing church in Africa. In February 1998 their monthly all-night Holy Ghost service at the Redemption Camp, 40 kilometres outside Lagos, attracted 250,000 worshippers. Within nine months the attendance reached one million, meeting on the first Friday of each month. On the 18th December 1998, while the US and UK were bombing Baghdad and the US Senate was debating whether to impeach President Clinton, I was privileged to be part of the platform party at a gathering of 7.2 million people at the Annual Special Holy Ghost Service at Lekki Beach near Lagos. This was, up to that point, the largest gathering of human beings in one place at one time in the history of the planet, yet CNN only mentioned the event briefly in its news broadcast, presumably because it was not as noteworthy as the bombing of Iraq or the political crisis in America.

Nigeria is a country with economic and political problems on a scale that is hard to comprehend when viewed from the perspective of the apparent wealth of Europe and the USA. Up to this point in Nigeria's recent history, no political leader had the ability to muster more than 25,000 people to attend a political rally, despite financial inducements or even coercion. Yet here, on this occasion at Lekki Beach, there was a passion that reflected the effect of the kingdom of God on the lives of the people who attended, an effect that compelled millions to want to spend a whole night and more in praise and worship of God. It placed a desire in my heart that a similar commitment would be found in the church in the West, with a similar outpouring of God's Holy Spirit, leading to a similar act of repentance from the church and a similar hunger for the extension of God's kingdom, especially in the UK.

The growth experienced by the African church is largely a result of breaking away from the format of traditional denominational churches planted by Western missionaries. In China the multiplication of house churches under a hostile Marxist government confounded missiologists, who expected the half-million believers left behind by retreating missionaries in 1948 to be crushed and persecuted out of existence. Most major cities in Latin America have seen an explosion of growth in churches pastored by staff with little or no formative training or experience with foreign mission agencies. This growth rate has largely come from those with a Pentecostal/Charismatic bias who have applied the foundational practices of the early church as described in the New Testament.

We have been trying to do something similar at the joint Anglican/Baptist church of St Thomas's in Sheffield, and in the chapters that follow I will explore our theological and biblical understanding of the gifts given by the Holy Spirit to the church and explain how we have applied them to nurture the members of our church. St Thomas's has experienced considerable growth, proportionally not dissimilar to the RCCG in Nigeria. In Nigeria the percentage of people who go to church is very high, whereas in the region of Sheffield less than 3 per cent attend church.[1] This makes what is happening at St Thomas's out of the ordinary in the UK, and my sincere hope is to share the principles we have discovered, so that members

---

[1] In a supplement to Peter Brierley's book *The Tide Is Running Out* (Christian Research, 2000), which gives more detail of regional church attendance, South Yorkshire is listed as having an average Sunday church attendance of 4.5 per cent, and it has been calculated from attendance returns that in Sheffield attendance is below 3 per cent.

of other churches around the country may also be nurtured for effective witness and ministry.

As I will explain in more detail in Chapter 1, St Thomas's operates as a Local Ecumenical Project (LEP). My experiences since joining the team as Baptist minister in January 1988 have helped to break down my previous suspicions of other traditions (see Chapter 2). By the time I arrived, the church had already integrated many of the values of Vineyard Ministries International (VMI) into its mission to Sheffield. The late John Wimber was the leader of VMI and came to the UK in the early 1980s. His conferences influenced many Anglican and Baptist churches, with his emphasis on the supernatural miracle-working power of the Holy Spirit to release and equip individuals in the church into effective evangelism and deeper commitment to Christ. See his books *Power Evangelism* (Hodder & Stoughton, 1985) and *Power Healing* (Hodder & Stoughton, 1986). My own personal encounter with VMI in 1986 was both experiential and theoretical, but lacked the dimension of practical outworking, so joining the team at St Thomas's provided a wonderful means for me to develop that practice, especially its emphasis on 'body ministry'.

Some might think that making such a move into an LEP would involve losing vital elements of my own Baptist heritage, and that the Anglicans would also be poorer as a result of such a merger. In fact, both sides have been enriched by the marriage. It has also enabled all of us to become more objective in our appreciation of the richness of the denominations which have shaped the way we worship and govern ourselves. Most denominations came into being as a result of conflict, and this has contributed over the years to a considerable hardening of attitudes between the different streams which make up the Christian church at large. This has hampered the work of the church, and the current climate of decline in the UK does not, in my opinion, permit the luxury of such infighting.

My pilgrimage thus far has enabled me to appreciate the richness and diversity of the church's different streams, and I have been surprised at the joy which can be found in celebrating the differences, rather than being continually at odds over fine points of doctrine which do not affect the salvation Jesus won for me on the cross. Given St Thomas's size and resources (our database indicates that we have over 2,500 members), we could easily opt out of the apparent restrictions of the traditional denominationalism we still represent and 'go it alone'. Such a path, however, would not bless the work God has done through those existing denominational structures, even with their weaknesses.

We are aware that it is not always profitable to preserve the traditions of the past in every detail just to maintain the status quo; nor is it productive to embrace every new whim in order to demonstrate that we are able to change for change's sake. Surely it is of greater importance to examine the Scriptures continually and adapt the methodology used by the early church to proclaim the unchanging message of the gospel and its historic truths to a world desperate for its life-changing power. Adaptability is indeed a crucial element – more than ever today, we are faced with the problem of communicating the gospel message to different generations with widely varying needs (see Chapter 3).

Undoubtedly, the success of St Thomas's has been greatly enhanced by the quality of leadership God has provided over the last 30 years. These leaders fostered a climate of openness and made the most of the membership's willingness to step out from some of the constraints of the institutional church structures and use methods considered by some to be unorthodox. The members, both past and present, should be applauded for putting such trust in their leaders and respecting them as people of integrity who were desirous of extending the kingdom rather than being driven by the latest trend in church politics.

The coming of Mike Breen in 1994 and his introduction of the Lifeskills programme (discussed in Chapter 7) has been the most fundamental change in this period and has created the language and vocabulary of the church's current theology and practice. This has resulted in a deeper awareness of the significance of the outworking of the rule of God through Christ. What has emerged is an easily transferable method of planned, disciplined and structured membership activity, at a personal as well as a corporate level, which has enabled members to comprehend more clearly how God reaches out to share his kingdom and grace in the context of intimate relationship.

I would also like to offer a fresh interpretation of the seminal passages in Romans 12, 1 Corinthians 12 and Ephesians 4 as the biblical basis for ministry at St Thomas's (see Chapters 4, 5 and 6). The expectation of the presence and influence of the Holy Spirit, understood in the way these texts imply, has produced for most people an atmosphere that is as natural as breathing air is essential to sustaining life.

Not all will agree with our interpretation of these passages, or with the apparently simplistic technique of tapping into a reservoir of unlimited power. Nonetheless, the interpretation is offered on the basis that it allows faith to be worked out creatively by using the relationship which all Christians have in common. For us at St Thomas's this has facilitated growth and created a community of believers who feel they 'belong' to one another as the family of God. Others may see the Lifeskills course as just another one of many discipleship programmes, which, if packaged in the right way, could have a measure of success. Nothing could be further from the truth. The essence of Lifeskills – the heart of what we do at St Thomas's – is to provide a framework for a way of living, in effect a Rule of Life (see Chapters 8 and 9). We believe it can offer to the wider church an accessible and adaptable model, and a valid option for growing a church.

1

An Anglican and Baptist Experiment

Coming together

St Thomas's has been a joint Anglican and Baptist church since 1982. The church came to terms with its mixed traditions in an unusual way, and from 1984 embraced much of the early theology and methodology of Vineyard Ministries International (VMI). The roots of this ecumenical marriage came about in 1978, when the Anglicans of St Thomas's shared the facilities of the local Crookes Baptist Church while extensive reordering of their own premises took place. The work took two years in all, and at that point neither church had any intention of merging their respective traditions, although they found they had many aspects in common.

It was only after the Anglicans had left for their newly ordered premises in 1980 that the two churches embarked on the process whereby they eventually agreed to become a Local Ecumenical Project (LEP). Normally such a project (in which each denomination continues to keep a separate register of its members) comes about when different denominations agree to share clergy, buildings and resources because continuing separately is not sustainable in the light of insufficient finance, changes in demographics or shrinking congregations. This was not so in the case of St Thomas's and Crookes. Both churches were healthily self-sustaining and moving forward into charismatic renewal, and could independently have carried out fruitful ministry to their communities. They came to recognise, however, that their combined strengths could lead to a stronger charismatic and evangelical presence in the local community and the city. In particular, early VMI methodology had already begun to enrich their worship by creating more space for the exercise of spiritual gifts. The practice of ministry in response to the message preached and/or to words of knowledge was encouraged and normative in both churches. Could they work together?

For many of the members at that time, denominational allegiance was often an accident of history. That is, the church tradition in which they had been reared determined the church they attended, rather than any strong conviction as to what was biblically or theologically important. A desire grew in both churches to celebrate their differences, while concentrating on those areas where there was a common mind. Discussion took place over a six-month period, during which the leaders and members' representatives from each fellowship addressed each church's approach to government, leadership, worship, evangelism and baptism. Apart from the last point, they discovered no major theological disagreements and what emerged was an enriching balance in most areas.

Both traditions, for example, recognised church government and leadership as being biblical and necessary for the building up of the body. Anglicans appeared to have a higher regard for ultimate pastoral authority residing in the leader (i.e. the vicar) of the local church, whereas Baptists, with their congregational form of government, seemed to lay more emphasis on the church members making decisions about the life and work of the church through their members' meetings. The conclusion of this particular debate was a desire both to avoid an unbiblical form of church democracy and to give current and future leaders the necessary freedom and authority to lead. The leaders, in turn, were to be supported and encouraged by an elected church council, made up of representatives from each denomination, which would act as a management group with responsibilities for fabric, finance and worship. Two Anglican wardens (a legal office and a requirement of Anglican canon law) and the Baptist church secretary (the senior lay position in Baptist churches) were to act as advisers and supervisors for denominational concerns.

Concerns about the apparent gulf between Anglican liturgical worship and the more spontaneous style of Baptist worship were happily discovered to be baseless. Indeed, the two approaches were seen to complement each other, especially as both churches were experimenting with the inclusion of spiritual gifts as they explored the charismatic dimension. Moreover, evangelism, as a biblical injunction, is enshrined in the tenets which govern both traditions. Article XVIII of the Thirty-Nine Articles of Religion states, 'For holy Scripture doth set out unto us only the Name of Jesus Christ, whereby men must be saved.'[1] This complements the Declaration of Principle of the Baptist Union of Great Britain's Constitution,

---

[1] *The Book of Common Prayer* (Eyre & Spottiswoode), p. 692.

which says that 'it is the duty of every disciple to bear personal witness to the Gospel of Jesus Christ, and to take part in the evangelisation of the world'.[2]

Of course, the issue of how to handle baptism was potentially the most difficult problem to resolve. The foundation of the solution was a desire to ensure that there was mutual respect for each tradition represented – not simply because it was tradition, but because the two forms of handling baptism grew out of sincerely held understanding of what the Scriptures say. The problems were primarily over the Anglican practice of infant baptism, although there were aspects of the Baptist approach which appeared defective to Anglicans. The historical roots of each tradition were helpful tools during this formative period. In particular, those who took part in the discussions recognised the need to apply the principle of freedom of conscience, one of the foundational concerns of the original Anabaptists. Without this mutual respect and the giving of freedom to others to follow their conscience, the LEP would not be able to operate effectively.

One rule that emerged out of the discussions on baptism was an agreement not to proselytise between each denomination. Both patterns of initiation were to be practised freely alongside each other. Those baptised as infants, but convinced of the rightness of believer's baptism, could (if they had not been confirmed as Anglicans) be baptised as believers. They then became Baptists within the LEP. Confirmation became the test in such cases in order to ensure an objective ruling rather than a subjective decision (such as it being thought pastorally appropriate),

---

[2] *The Baptist Union Directory for 1991–92* (Gem Publishing Company, 1992), p. 9.

and seemed a less difficult route to follow. Confirmation was recognised as a public acknowledgement of the validity of baptismal vows taken on by others on the candidate's behalf in
infancy, and seemed an appropriate point of no return. Those
who, having been confirmed, could not accept the renewal of
baptismal vows allowed in Anglican liturgy as being sufficient,
or who could not, as the Prayer Book puts it, 'quiet their conscience', were not allowed to be baptised as believers within the
LEP. Similarly, those from a Baptist background who desired
Anglican confirmation could not be sanctioned within the LEP.
In each case matters were to be dealt with as appropriate
denominational pastoral issues.

The LEP was formally brought into being in 1982. Robert
Warren, the Anglican vicar at the time, commented, 'It felt as if
we were putting back together two halves of a valuable, but
fragile, work of art that had somehow been tragically broken.'[3]
Unwittingly, his leadership and the inauguration of the LEP
laid the foundation for the current growth of the church. St
Thomas's has for many years been recognised as a city-wide
church as well as retaining a parish emphasis – it is still, after
all, technically an Anglican parish church, but it is also now the
largest church in the north of England.

By the time I arrived at St Thomas's, the coming together of
both churches had passed through a few crises regarding leadership, which had resulted in some staff members leaving,
including my predecessor, whose contract had come to an end.
The church had grown to over 650 members and the Nine
O'Clock Service (NOS) was in full swing, attracting about 300
worshippers. The story of their demise is not pertinent to this

---

[3] Robert Warren, *In the Crucible* (Highland Books, 1989), p. 153.

book. Suffice it to say at this juncture they were very orthodox
in their theology and like the rest of St Thomas's greatly influenced by the ministry of John Wimber. By 1991 they had physically left St Thomas's. The structures used to facilitate growth
through three congregations were each led by a staff member
with a dedicated leadership team. The 9.15 a.m. attracted
mostly young families, the 11.15 a.m. had an older congregation and the 6.30 p.m. (which I led) had approximately 350
young people, with an average age of 25 years, of which 83 per
cent were in small groups. Anglican and Baptist forms of
worship were reflected in all three congregations and did not
seem to present any real difficulties to the membership.

A new way forward

For a decade the new joint structures served St Thomas's well
under the team led by Robert Warren. Further changes followed in October 1993, when Robert moved on to serve the
wider church. Within six months of his departure, the Anglican
vicar Mike Breen was appointed as team leader. His background suited the peculiar structures of the church. His previous experience included serving as youth leader in the city of
Cambridge, and it was during this period that he embraced the
theological values of VMI. There followed a productive ministry in a London inner-city parish, where the church grew from
40 members to 250 in three years. He later accepted the position of teacher–pastor at the Southern Baptist Church, Indian
Hills, Little Rock, Arkansas, and went on to be Assistant to the
Dean of Little Rock Episcopal Cathedral.

After accepting the call to St Thomas's, Mike sensed the
Lord impressing on him the word 'Ephesus'. During the six

months prior to taking up his responsibilities, he researched the theme, weighing up the implications against his own extensive experience, and comparing it with the previous history of St Thomas's. The location of Ephesus in the time of Paul meant that it had the role of principal city of its region, and under the apostle's leadership it was used as a base for the evangelisation of Asia Minor. Luke records that Paul taught and trained local leaders and believers in a rented building, the hall of Tyrannus (Acts 19). From this centre, teams were sent out to plant churches at Smyrna, Pergamum, Thyatira, Philadelphia, Sardis, Laodicea and Colosse. From this base, the text states, Paul exercised a powerful ministry, and 'God did extraordinary miracles . . . the Jews and Greeks . . . were all seized with fear . . . the word of the Lord spread widely and grew in power' (Acts 19:11, 17, 20). Mike came to the following conclusion concerning the interpretation of the word 'Ephesus' for his calling to St Thomas's in Sheffield – the fourth largest city in England, and the principal city for its region. In giving him the word 'Ephesus', Mike believed God was

> declaring something that had already occurred but it was also something that he desired to develop in the future. The church of St Thomas's was to function as a resource to its city and region. It was to be a base for church planting and mission and a centre for teaching and training.[4]

When Mike arrived at the church, he and I (as the Baptist minister) were the only ordained clergy in the leadership, the three other ordained team members having dispersed to different

---

[4] Mike Breen, *The Body Beautiful* (Monarch, 1997), p. 25.

churches. We agreed, however, to wait for at least six months after his installation before appointing any extra members of staff, in order to allow space and time to discuss the implications of his research and to discern how the Ephesus vision could be implemented.

As is the case in any organisation when a new phase begins, the new way forward proved to involve a significant and radical departure from the church's previous way of functioning. It was not that the previous leadership style had been wrong, but rather that a productive chapter in the life of St Thomas's had come to a natural end. The former style had operated on a consensus model, whereby most activities progressed through papers being raised by members of staff concerning policy changes or outreach initiatives, ideas which were then processed through the church council. By the time of Mike's arrival, these procedures had in many ways become stifled, impaired and over-bureaucratic. Fresh eyes recognised the need for re-evaluation if the new way forward was to take shape successfully.

Lifeskills

The following three years involved a reorientation of the church council, wardens, leaders of small groups and church members towards a more directive form of leadership. This was achieved largely through what is currently called the Lifeskills course (discussed in more detail in Chapter 7). This unpacks the requirement for operating on a three-dimensional level: having a strong and vital relationship with God (UP), enjoying good relationships with members of the church (IN), and relating to the world in which members live (OUT). Most church traditions operate on a two-dimensional level. Evangelicals and charismatics tend to have a strong emphasis on UP and IN, while OUT is often only expressed in occasional 'revival' or crusade events. Roman Catholic and High Church streams tend to emphasise the UP and OUT aspects and lack the intimacy of the IN. Liberals tend towards IN and OUT, while the UP aspect is frequently construed as confused and indistinct.

Initially only those who were closest to the centre of the church's leadership worked through the course. Then it was opened to each of the remaining levels of leadership and became the means whereby they were able to determine their own personal ministry and how it could be used to progress the mission in the church. Within 18 months, the course was made available to all members, and it has now become the vocabulary of St Thomas's theology and practice. It has been particularly helpful in affirming the worth of members of the body at personal, small group and cluster level, as well as in the marketplace. The main emphasis at the outset was to capitalise on the gifting that God, through the Holy Spirit, had already imparted to all members, while at the same time highlighting deficiencies and finding constructive ways of addressing them.

For many this was the beginning of a time of liberation into a new way of doing church, because the emphasis was now on every member clearly identifying their role and function in the church, using the format of Lifeskills. For some, however, the fundamental change in approach and new leadership style proved too difficult to adjust to, and in the first 18 months about 200 people left to worship in other local churches that were more traditional in their ecclesiology and thus better suited to their temperaments.

New structures, new styles

The transition for the church family from the previous style of leadership to the new style came at a point when there was a 'hunger for authority', as Richard John Neuhaus describes it in his *Freedom for Ministry*.[5] The departure of the members of the previous team had naturally left a vacuum in terms of authority, in that their responsibility ceased when they left and a new way of operating appropriate to the change of leadership needed to be bedded in. The vision of the kingdom of God and the outworking of it, which had been a strong emphasis within the church through the influence of VMI, needed to be restated to a generation who were not properly conversant with the implications of Jesus' proclamation that the kingdom of God was at hand and his call to repentance (Mark 1:14–15). Neuhaus points out from this text that 'the kingdom of God is the indicative, repentance the imperative', and that the 'therefore' of the gospel needs to be spelt out clearly. The commitment of the church membership to the imperative of walking out their faith in this manner had begun to wane by this point, and the matter needed to be addressed so that they could recapture their 'first love', as Jesus had warned the church at Ephesus (Revelation 2:1–7).

The new way forward led to us following a pattern of operation which C. Peter Wagner has helpfully clarified in his book *The New Apostolic Churches*.[6] Under this schema, authority structures were redefined, worship patterns and styles were

---

[5] Richard John Neuhaus, *Freedom for Ministry* (HarperCollins, 1979), pp. 197–8.

[6] C. Peter Wagner, *The New Apostolic Churches* (Regal, 1998), pp. 19–25.

re-evaluated, clearer teaching on financial obligations was given to the membership, leadership training was adapted to meet the demands of church life, and outreach was seen to be the responsibility of all. Ministry focused more on the gifts given by the Holy Spirit to enable the body to function in the ways we believed God intended for the new phase.

Prayer focus was lifted to a new level, and this has continued. Currently there are five times of prayer each weekday, led by members of staff and using a cathedral and monastic format of morning and evening prayers: 7.00 a.m. Lauds, 9.00 a.m. Terce, Noon, 3.00 p.m. Sext, and 7.00 p.m. Vespers. Quarterly whole nights of prayer, using the format of the RCCG in Nigeria, allow more space for praise, celebration, testimony and preaching. The hardest part of these all-night events is breaking through the period between 1.00 and 3.00 a.m., when the body and spirit long to be curled up in bed. This, the darkest part of the night, becomes for some a major struggle. However, when the realisation comes that the night is now 'far gone', it becomes obvious that there is more to be gained by staying than leaving. From this point on, an extraordinary breakthrough in the intensity of prayer and pouring out of God's Spirit seems to happen, evidenced by healings and prophetic ministry. Those who have attended such occasions all attest to having their faith lifted to a new level. Some members have felt oil, with an attendant aroma, dripping from their hands, and people have been healed by their touch. On another occasion a non-Christian young man came in to see what was happening and was so overwhelmed by the power of God's presence that he came to faith. Without exception, people come away from such gatherings with a greater sense of awe for the God who has called them to share in his kingdom.

This resulted in a re-examination of what changes were necessary for the church to further the mission of God. One of Mike Breen's early sermon series concentrated on Jesus' message to the seven churches in Revelation, using the negative instructions as well as the positive in order to determine what he wanted from them. The foundational principles of the doctrine of grace, central to all the processes of a believer's life, were coupled with the implications of the covenant God made with his people in terms of its application to the corporate life of the church. From this perspective 'mission' was described as incorporating the whole of the church's ministry – locally and in the city and country, not just overseas. Each year that passes calls for greater financial commitment in order to advance mission in this way.

New leadership

From this point onward, part of what Charles Van Engen describes in *God's Missionary People* as 'theology-on-the-way' became the norm.[7] This involved looking at the methodology of other traditions as to how the church engaged with mission corporately and at a personal level, and then applying it to St Thomas's. We were now at a point where we could move on from the previous, slow-moving consensus model of operation, replacing it as planned with a more directive style of leadership to reflect the New Testament form of church. The use of policy papers and lengthy debate was finally discontinued. Instead, leaders appointed and anointed for particular tasks were allowed to exercise the power and authority necessary to do those tasks effectively – through the empowering of the Holy

---

[7] Charles Van Engen, *God's Missionary People* (Baker, 1991), p. 21.

Spirit gained by prayer, counsel and accountability. In this way, we believed the church would be enabled to carry out its wider mission.

This new style of leadership was introduced on the basis that leaders in the Scriptures had a commission under God to lead the church in order to empower the membership to function as a body, rather than operating as mere employees of the church. In my own Baptist tradition, however, there are situations in which leaders are unable to function in such a directive leadership role because the members prefer to make all the policy decisions, in a mistaken interpretation of the statement, 'Each church has the liberty, under the guidance of the Holy Spirit, to interpret and administer His Laws.'[8] In some cases churches have dismissed a pastor who, in their opinion, disagreed with their oversight.

At St Thomas's, those who favoured the consensus approach to church government (which was how the church was governed previously) initially resisted this feature of the Apostolic paradigm church. Mike countered this by appealing to the charge given to him by the bishop at his installation as the Anglican vicar of the church as having the 'cure of souls', a technical term in canon law. Within the meaning of the law, this includes responsibility for worship, preaching and the sacraments, as well as for those on the electoral roll of the parish.

On this premise, Mike's leadership was recognised and agreed to by senior clergy, assistant clergy and other members of staff, who all indicated their willingness to be directly accountable to him in his role as team leader. This initially appeared to set the tone for abuse of power and autocratic leadership. However, the

---

[8] *The Baptist Union Directory for 1991–92*, p. 9.

desire was to clarify who and what the role of a leader was and remain true to the biblical emphasis of the office. Appropriate mechanisms were set in place to ensure accountability was exercised effectively and, under Mike's leadership, the church council and officers required by the two denominations were to function in a similar way to the deacons appointed by the apostles in Acts 7, with finance, stewardship and fabric being their principal areas of concern. As an elected body, they were also to act as a 'boundary control commission', to allow the membership's response to the church's mission to be represented and heard in a pastorally sensitive way. Included on the council today are the elected representatives of the cluster groups (see below), two Anglican wardens as the bishop's representatives, and a Baptist warden representing the Baptist church members' meeting. Staff are ex-officio members of the council.

The reordered church

Two years after Mike Breen's arrival a major rationalisation of church life began to take shape and is extant today. Membership requirements are defined by attendance at the Sunday celebration service and membership of a small group (or cell). These small groups are also formed into clusters (or congregations) of three to seven cells. Clusters now meet as 'missional communities', mainly on Sundays, in different parts of the city. The Alpha course developed by Holy Trinity, Brompton, is part of the introduction to the values of the church, and this is followed by a Beta (Membership) course that describes the church's understanding of evangelism and mission, healing and counselling, initiation, membership, and vocation within the body. The latter session is a condensed version of the Lifeskills course and all members are also

encouraged to attend the full course in order to be conversant
with the vocabulary of the church. Denominational affiliation
is considered secondary to conversion and integration into the
body.

This reordering of the church's approach laid the foundation
for an influx of the postmodern generation (or Generation X),
for whom such a format is readily accessible, and who now form
the bulk of the current membership. During the Alpha and
Beta courses, participants are incorporated into small groups
within the church family. Initiation, either by confirmation as
Anglicans or by believer's baptism, is strongly encouraged,
although there is little pressure from the staff, in recognition of
the post-denominational aspect of the Xer generation, for
whom allegiance to anything institutional is suspect and to be
avoided. (The different generational needs will be examined in
more detail in Chapter 3.)

Mission, as mentioned above, was redefined to include all the
activities of the church. The charge given by Jesus to his disciples to be witnesses in Jerusalem, Judea, Samaria and the
uttermost parts of the earth needed to be interpreted into
accessible language for this new phase of the church's life. Thus
mission came to be described as applying to the *community*, *city*,
country and *continents* (known as 'the 4 Cs'). The intention was
to counter the popular view of mission being limited to people
working outside the UK, whom the church paid and supported
for undertaking such 'mission work' on their behalf. This is
sometimes described as a form of 'cheque book Christianity'.

The new policy was to consider all those working at home or
overseas on behalf of the church as having the status of staff
members, who should in turn reflect the new values of the
church. When this policy was implemented, there were nine

people working overseas. St Thomas's agreed to continue supporting them under the terms on which they had originally gone out from the church. As soon as they came back on furlough, they were advised of the changes in policy. As it transpired, all but one were within two years of finishing their contracts with the respective agencies for whom they worked. The last person concluded his ministry in 1999. Currently there are no personnel engaged in traditional mission work overseas.

The aim of this new mission procedure was to improve accountability and pastoral coverage for those sent out, by creating a more meaningful relationship with the church that had commissioned them. The previous policy regarding personnel sent out to minister to the wider church had been to leave the sponsoring agencies to perform this service. Such a policy, however, seemed to lack integrity and proper accountability, and was deemed inconsistent with the way the church now viewed mission. There was also the issue of the theological emphasis of some of the sponsoring agencies now being at odds with St Thomas's as the sending church, particularly given its increasing emphasis on the work of the Spirit.

Under the influence of this reordering of church priorities and outlook, there developed a desire to consolidate St Thomas's work and vision in the local community (our Jerusalem) and the city (our Judea). It seemed to us that sending personnel beyond those boundaries while the work closer to home was deficient was inconsistent with kingdom principles. Under the previous leadership, the church had used the resources from God in ways which were appropriate for that era. Now, with the impetus of Mike Breen's Ephesus vision and a clearer understanding of the '4 Cs' of mission, it seemed imperative to ensure that the church was strong and influential in the community and the city, before we moved out to the rest of the country and the continents.

Serving the city vision

Today St Thomas's database indicates a membership of 2,500 people, and 85 per cent are under the age of 40. Out of these several thousand people, only 298 regard themselves as Anglicans, and 188 as Baptists. These statistics reflect the post-modern and post-denominational characteristics of those who form the bulk of our membership. The size of St Thomas's is hugely significant in contrast to general church attendance in the region, which is less than 3 per cent. In the 2002 Diocesan Handbook of Sheffield, the average parish church attendance is given as 25 worshippers, and many churches have no young people attending their services at all. Such churches will inevitably close over time, because there will be no one to replace the ageing congregations. Why and how has St Thomas's bucked the trend?

I believe the answer lies primarily in our city vision. From September 1998, in order to serve the needs of this vision, we began to meet in a leisure centre on one Sunday each month. This innovation facilitated growth mostly from unchurched folk, because the venue was more accessible than the parish church and there was considerably more space. It was recognised from the start, however, that it would only be a temporary home. The premises were only available for about 35 Sundays a year, it was costly, and having to set up and dismantle the equipment each week was an added burden.

We were therefore delighted when, in January 2000, we were given the chance to rent a disused Roxy nightclub in the city centre. It had previously been known as a 'palace of sin', of course, and its infamous reputation had spread far and wide. Using it as a place of worship attracted much media attention, which resulted in a considerable amount of free publicity. In the first six weeks 400 people were added to the church.

The services at the parish church in Crookes continued to provide morning worship for those committed to the local community, and were attended by approximately 300 people. Sunday morning meetings in the city focused on seeing the kingdom of God breaking through in the workplace – that is, the place where members spend most of their time during the week. This has proven to be a fertile ground for the work of the kingdom, and a survey revealed the workplace as their most productive and effective ground for witnessing. Most of the worshippers at the morning service were in the 35–55 age bracket (the generation known as Baby Boomers).

For the younger generation, the Xers, the evening celebration service became a magnet. Its structure was defined by the mission vision of its small groups and clusters, designed to release people to be a relevant church to their world. Clusters also began to plant missional communities among students, the café culture, the art culture, inner-city areas, and Gen X singles and married couples. The worship pattern during our last year of occupancy at the Roxy used three out of the four Sunday services to focus on the central Lifeskills concepts of UP, IN and OUT. UP included experimental styles of worship, creative ways of listening and responding to God's word, and preaching which incorporated video, audiovisual presentations and popular music. IN used the medium of thanksgiving testimonies from clusters which reflected both their small groups and their wider mission. We prayed specifically for them, and worked through issues raised in the cluster groups within the context of the service itself. OUT was a time to reconsider practically their spiritual act of worship, and involved literally going out from the venue for a period of time into bars and cafés in the city centre as part of the celebration service.

Operating at this level sometimes required a great degree of flexibility, and there was also a tendency to be carried away by the apparent success of growing the church. In January 2001, Mike Breen felt he had a direct word from the Lord posing this challenging question: 'What would you do if I took the Roxy away from you?' This seemed to conflict with the current pattern of events. We were at an advanced stage of negotiations with the owners to buy the building. Jack Nicholls, the Bishop of Sheffield, and his staff had given official permission for it to be used as a place of worship, and the city planners had raised no objections.

The staff discussed and prayed over the situation with Mike, trying to discern what such a turnaround in our plans would involve. What *would* we do if we lost the Roxy? We had always planned to phase in the process of planting out clusters as missional communities as our numbers grew, and some had already been experimenting by meeting in alternative venues. Part of the reasoning behind the planting out of such communities was the need of space for growth at the morning and evening celebrations. Should we bring the plans forward? By the time autumn came, however, there was no indication that we needed to speed up the pace, although the city cluster leaders had begun to make appropriate plans.

Then, in December 2001, one of our members, who had reservations about some of the heaters used in the Roxy building, contacted the fire department and the health and safety executive with the best of intentions, concerned to ensure that the equipment was legal. Inspection revealed that in order to conform to current legislation over £60,000 needed to be spent on updating the electrical cabling and other features of the building. The owners were unwilling to spend such a sum, and the church leadership did not think it was a wise use of our own resources. This was, we realised, confirmation of the word given to Mike. It was time to implement the alternative plans we had made over the previous 12 months.

On the 27th January 2002 the last celebrations were held at the Roxy. The final gathering was used as a commissioning service to send 17 missional communities into the city. The Bishop of Sheffield was very supportive and sympathetic to the reasons why we had to move out in this way, and his staff smoothed the path in those parishes where the new communities were to meet, helping to avoid any perception of threat to existing parish work.

Our belief that we had followed a clear word from God was confirmed by the fact that a greater number of people were coming to faith after we had moved out into the missional communities than when we had met in the Roxy. Today the church still needs a base for its city mission, and we are awaiting God's direction on how we might best progress with this aspect of the church's Ephesus vision.

Another option on offer for members takes place at the parish church, using the form of a teaching service that meets the needs of those looking for more in-depth Bible study to help them in their mission of extending God's kingdom. This attracts adult members of all ages. The first hour is devoted to worship, and includes opportunity and literal space for prayer ministry (a section of the worship area is cleared of chairs to permit people to kneel, lie down or move about). After a break for refreshments, there is an expository sermon. This helps in the process of recognising the different styles of learning and is a practical means of demonstrating how, over the generations, people have developed their faith.

To facilitate a whole-church perspective, especially after the loss of the Roxy, on the second Sunday of each month the format of the day is changed in order to bring everyone together. The day begins with early morning Holy Communion at the parish church. Clusters are then encouraged to organise events at different venues to help foster deeper relationships. For some this takes the form of sharing brunch together, walking, swimming, bowling, or reading the Sunday news-papers together with coffee and pastries, etc. The afternoon activities start at 4.00 p.m. at the Octagon Centre of the University of Sheffield and include a programme for children to run concurrently with the adult seminars. The day concludes with an evening celebration, which updates the whole church family on the outworking of St Thomas's vision.

Serving the region as an Ephesus-style church

As a continuation of the Ephesus call to the church, and to facilitate the current and future mission of St Thomas's, we were also required to share our resources willingly with the wider Christian community. At Ephesus, Paul concentrated his ministry in the city at the hall of Tyrannus, where he trained church-planters and leaders. It became a centre where people could gather and from which they could go out and make dis-ciples, as directed in the Great Commission. The principle was put into practice at St Thomas's through my appointment as

Director of Mission, with the task of developing relationships with local, regional and overseas churches and their leaders.

The Director of Mission role – with a senior staff member appointed to the post – was created to demonstrate to the church membership and to other churches in the area that the sharing of our resources is a priority on our agenda. Other churches are offered the opportunity to network with St Thomas's, and thus to draw on its resources. For some smaller churches this means joining St Thomas's at the Second Sunday Celebrations mentioned above. For others it involves a team visit from St Thomas's to help train their church to share similar values – a process that includes an audit of the church's life and work. Sometimes the leader of a church uses the network for personal fellowship and support. Leaders' days are held quarterly for network churches, with the aim of continuing to encourage and equip them. The three-day.leaders' consultations held twice annually have the same purpose. The Lifeskills syllabus is used as the vocabulary of all those churches that consider themselves part of the network. Individuals, teams, clusters and small groups are also utilised in helping to resource these churches. Currently there are in excess of 70 churches that consider themselves part of the network.

One leader in the diocese who is thoroughly evangelical and charismatic in his theology looks upon the network as a haven in which he can truly be at ease. His frustration takes the form of having to continually apologise even to colleagues in his chapter meeting who are conservative evangelical but not in sympathy with his charismatic bias. The encouragement he receives by being part of the network helps relieve a degree of the stress he feels.

From time to time, teams from St Thomas's visit churches

around the world to minister to them, as well as to learn from them. These teams report back to the church in Sheffield with prayer needs and points of thanksgiving. Occasionally, leaders from international network churches visit St Thomas's to see first hand how our theological and biblical principles are applied. International churches which are currently part of the network involve Nigeria, Nepal, Sarawak, Indonesia, France, Ireland, Switzerland and the USA. Salaries are paid for a pastor in Nigeria, an overseer and ten church-planters and evangelists in Nepal, a seminary professor in Indonesia, and a pastor in Turkey. The emphasis is on building relationships within the wider body, and the same principles of mutual support and encouragement are applied to the international network.

2

Pride and Prejudice

St Thomas's Church, as will be clear from the previous chapter, has been on a journey of discovery for many years now. It has not been an easy or painless process, but every individual involved has undertaken his or her own personal spiritual journey, and, like the church itself, many have ended up in a completely different place from where they started. I am no exception. Before we move on to examine some of the central principles behind St Thomas's approach, I feel it is important to tell some of my own story in order to demonstrate how a fundamental reassessment of a person's understanding, methodology and theology can come about, and also to explain how I came to be involved with St Thomas's.

Early tendencies

The wholesale change in my outlook had begun to take shape before I joined St Thomas's, but for many years prior to that, I had seen things in an entirely different way. In an extreme contrast with the St Thomas-style approach I later embraced, my youth was set against the background of Calvinism and Ulster Protestant fundamentalism. I was converted through Youth for Christ at the age of 12, and my formative years as a Christian began in the evangelical surroundings of Irish Methodism at the Grosvenor Hall, also known as the Belfast Central Mission, which had a worshipping community of over 2,000. I shall always be grateful to the leaders who accepted that my decision to be a follower of Christ was a serious and mature one, in spite of my young age. I was quickly integrated into the life of the Mission, and the Young People's Christian Endeavour was particularly influential in building up my faith.

The innocence and insecurity of youth, along with the lack of a formal secondary education, fostered within me a desire for authenticity in the outworking of my Christian faith. To this end, I was mentored by several significant individuals in my early teenage years, and was encouraged to read works by fundamentalist and Calvinistic authors. These certainly met my desire to be schooled in 'sound doctrine', and from an early age I was more theologically aware than my peers. Inevitably, however, my concentration on 'soundness' resulted in a Pharisaic form of Christianity, which is often the hallmark of conservative evangelicals.

After I enlisted in the Royal Navy at the age of 17, there followed 23 years of service with an intense involvement in the Naval Christian Fellowship, a para-church movement similar to the Universities and Colleges Christian Fellowship (UCCF). The father figures of this movement were deeply influenced by the Protestant work ethic and conservative evangelicalism, and they had a strong Puritan bias. During this period my earlier Pharisaic tendencies were reinforced by the kind of theological

reading I was encouraged to undertake, and by self-education
in Reformed theology.

With such a background, my faith became a form of legalistic religious consumerism. The more meetings I could attend,
the more theological and Christian books I could read, the
more I could hang out with other Christians, especially the
'super' types, the more I hoped some kind of impartation would
take place that would make me 'more spiritual'. This preoccupation with information-gathering included a constant personal analysis, which I deduced would enable me to determine
truth and reality and their application for my life. It was as if
God was looking over my shoulder at everything I did, point-
ing out the deficiencies of my actions or attitudes and uttering
that old phrase from school reports, 'could do better'.

I now realise that this simply tapped into my own insecurity
and masked an inability – even an unwillingness – to discern
intellectually and experientially what Christ, by his Spirit,
desired to do in my life. For the most part, I believed in the truth
of the Scriptures as the rule and guide for my life, I lived a moral
and upright life, I attended church regularly and heard those
truths preached faithfully. Nonetheless, there was a rigidity in
my life that acted as an emotional straitjacket and seemed to
lack liberty of spirit.

Prospects for ministry

The next stage of the process came about during my training
for the ordained ministry in the Baptist Church at Spurgeon's
College during the early 1980s. In the first year my New
Testament tutor unwittingly fired my imagination as we studied
the Sermon on the Mount and kingdom ethics. I realised for the

first time that the text was a description of the lifestyle of a disciple, and not a detailed format for living in a prescribed way in order to gain the favour of God. The more the text was unpacked during the seminars, the more difficult I found it to conceive how such a church would look when its members operated in this way. I reasoned, however, that being trained to serve and lead as a pastor was bound to equip me as a vital instrument to the church in this regard. I would learn what it was all about over the next few years. In addition, to be called and empowered to proclaim such a message, with its attendant social implications and expectation of the miraculous as shown in the ministry of the early apostles, seemed an exciting prospect with which to begin my pastoral ministry.

At the end of my three years' training, however, I was still not sure whether I fully understood what was implied by Jesus' description in Matthew 5–7 of members of his kingdom, who, with their changed hearts and radical lifestyles, acted in such marked contrast to the religious establishment of their day. Even on a casual observation, the modern church at large – including my own Baptist denomination – did not appear to be overtly committed to proclaiming such a radical message. Instead, the traditional denominations seemed to be more committed to organised religion and maintenance of the status quo.

The charismatics in the UK at that time did appear to have a glimmer of the anticipation of the work of the kingdom I now sought. They seemed, however, to be more locked into the 'second blessing' theology of classical Pentecostalism, with a heightened emphasis on the spectacular gifts of the Spirit such as glossolalia, prophecy and words of knowledge. Biblical teaching often tended to be from selected texts which were used to bolster their plea for more emphasis on the supernatural, and this did not rest easy with my search for a way through.

Part of the training pattern at Spurgeon's College was that one student each year was selected to spend a year on the staff of First Baptist Church, Dallas, Texas, as the British minister. I was invited to accept the position, which, as an Irishman, I found ironic! The church was larger than life in every respect. It had a membership roll of 26,000 and five buildings in downtown Dallas, as well as two multi-storey car parks. The budget for the year I was there, 1983–84, was 11 million dollars, and they had vast resources to further the church's ministry.

Spending time in a Southern Baptist church helped to consolidate some of my fundamentalist tendencies, and its apparently successful mission, built largely around programmes, seemed to me to be a good model to emulate. I recognised that in the UK this would present some difficulties, as the church at home was not as wealthy or influential as the church in the USA, but at least it was something positive to aim for. One particular lesson I learnt that was transferable to any setting was that every time the gospel was preached, no matter how confused or eloquent the delivery, space should always be given for people to make a response. This is a practice I still employ.

Pastoral concerns

After a year in Dallas I returned to the UK to seek settlement in a Baptist church. I had made a covenant with God to serve him in an area where the evangelical witness and Baptist presence was low. This seemed to indicate the north of England, and in December 1984 I duly accepted a call to be the pastor of Durham City Baptist Church.

Even though, at the age of 43, I was mature in years at the time of my ordination, my inexperience of the constraints, practicalities and responsibilities involved in the post brought me a mixture of elation and disappointment during my first four years in the pastorate. I had an expectation that the church should naturally grow and become 'salt and light', so that it would be self-evident the kingdom of God was being advanced through the correct kind of teaching and preaching in which I had been schooled. It seemed to me, however, that the practice of appropriate pastoral visiting and 'being there' for the members was not working out in the people's lives – or, for that matter, in my own – in the manner described in the Sermon on the Mount.

In hindsight, I realise this was a crisis of confidence in my own faith. There was no doubt I had been faithful to the call to ordination, and good, honest men and women had validated that call through interviews and godly counsel. The fact that I had come through training at one of the finest theological colleges in the land and had gained a degree meant I had satisfied an appropriate learned body that I understood theology and had a good knowledge of the Scriptures. Had I applied the same energy to engineering, chemistry or some other subject, I felt that I would have been able to show the appropriate professionalism and competency in the results I produced. Yet here I was, in possession of the most powerful message the world has ever known, and I was unable to demonstrate that it worked in the way described in the New Testament.

A paradigm shift

My reading of John Wimber's book *Power Evangelism* in 1986 was the beginning of the paradigm shift in outlook which led at last to an appreciation of the essence of the Sermon on the Mount seminars given by my New Testament tutor at Spurgeon's College. Wimber's reasoning served to heighten my expectation that when the word was preached and people met in the name of Jesus, signs and wonders under the influence and empowering of the Holy Spirit should follow. Wimber argued that this accords with the Greek word *semeia*, defined as 'a sign (as a rule, visually perceived, but occasionally also heard) by which one recognises a particular person or thing, a confirmatory, corroborative, authenticating mark or token'.[1] Using VMI's format and practice of worship, proclamation of the word and ministry proved to be a helpful model in working out the reality of such emphasis in those early days.

I discovered that the teachings of VMI satisfied the desire for authenticity and integrity in matters of faith that had been instilled in my youth. In particular, John Wimber's thesis differed from the 'second blessing' emphasis of the charismatic movement's neo-Pentecostalism whereby speaking in tongues was the definitive evidence of being filled with the Holy Spirit. In spite of being conditioned by Reformed theology, I did not subscribe to the view that some of the gifts of the Holy Spirit ceased at the end of the apostolic age, when the canon of Scripture was agreed, and Wimber's viewpoint concurred with the biblical text as I read it. He described the activity of the Holy Spirit as 'the consummate charismatic experience . . . and any ensuing interaction between the individual and the Holy Spirit comes under the heading of "fillings" as taught by Paul.

---

[1] O. Hoifus, '*Semeion,* sign, wonder, miracle', in Colin Brown (ed.), *The Dictionary of New Testament Theology* Vol. 2 (Paternoster Press, 1976), pp. 626–27.

Further, these fillings may happen again and again – they are both initiatory and repeatable.'[2]

The church, he contended, should aim to serve the God of the Bible, who still performed miracles, by broadening the concept of a 'power encounter' to include any event in which the kingdom of God confronts the kingdom of this world, particularly by evangelism, healings and exorcisms. The challenge Wimber posed to traditional denominations was the same as that posed by Veli Matti Kärkkäinen, that 'the church was "instituted" by Christ and "constituted" by the Spirit . . . and should live in a continual Pentecost',[3] not unlike that described in the Acts of the Apostles. The expectation of the church should be to experience God and his power at work, and not just to talk about moral improvement in the lives of Christians or church politics.

Such teaching caused me to take a fresh look at my own practice in church. Contrary to the theological perspectives I had habitually followed, I now saw that it was not the be-all and end-all to make sure that everything was done in a regulated way. I had been taught that, when preparing Sunday worship, it was correct to allow the period of worship to last for no more than an hour and a quarter, to choose the right hymns, to include the notices and the offering at the most appropriate moments, and to leave a good space for the sermon. Behind this, I think, was a hope that people would comment particularly on the edifying and sound nature of the sermon, thus giving me assurance that the research and time spent in its prep-

---

[2] John Wimber, *Power Evangelism* (Hodder & Stoughton, 1985), p. 141.

[3] Veli Matti Kärkkäinen, 'Towards a Theology and Ecclesiology of the Spirit', *Journal of Pentecostal Theology*, Issue 14 (1999), p. 79.

aration had been justified. I must stress that there is nothing intrinsically wrong with such motives, but an emphasis on regulation generally leads to lifeless worship.

In November 1986 I attended my first series of VMI seminars, and the experience led to a paradigm shift in my theology. By then our whole family had been affected by VMI's teachings, and I felt a new elation, but also a greater degree of uncertainty within me. I had accepted the call to the Durham church on a conservative evangelical ticket, and now this shift in my outlook involved changes for them and for me.

Within two weeks my younger son, Keith, gave me a prophecy. It indicated that I would move from the traditional Baptist system to a church – still somewhere in the north of England – which would reflect Vineyard principles. In addition, it would come about that we would be together as a family, worshipping at the same church. At that stage I had no idea how this would work out in practice, and there was no immediate reason for me to leave Durham. To be together as a family was highly desirable, as my naval career had made a stable and continuous family life problematic, but it seemed a remote possibility at that juncture. Keith was leaving to work in London, and our eldest son Nigel, a Royal Navy dentist, had just been appointed to serve in Brunei. Perhaps, I speculated, it meant that the family would be together when my wife Mary and I reached retirement.

A practice shift

Over the next six months I filed this prophecy in my memory under 'not sure, but interesting', and continued the work of processing the shift in my theology at a personal level, seeking also to explain my new understanding of the work and person of the Holy Spirit to the Durham fellowship. They were very tolerant.

In May 1997 my Area Superintendent, John Nicholson, approached me with an invitation to move from Durham. It was not that my current ministry was in trouble or that the fellowship had problems with my ministry style – John knew of the changes that had taken place in my encounter with God and was very supportive of the way things were developing at the church. He asked if I knew about St Thomas's Church in Sheffield. My initial response was that I knew little about it, but it sounded like an ecumenical situation and was therefore of no interest to me. I also told him I was not looking to move to another church. John persisted, however, and described how St Thomas's vicar Robert Warren had been responsible for inviting John Wimber and his team to the north of England two years in succession. It did sound interesting, but my prejudice towards such arrangements was quite profound at this stage, and to contemplate working with Anglicans seemed like a 'theological bridge too far'.

Yet John knew this was a definite call from God to me, and he pressed home the fact that this church needed a strong Baptist minister to help build up its small membership – a Baptist minister, moreover, who was both evangelical and charismatic in theology, as well as being ecumenically minded. Much to my surprise, he was convinced that I fitted the profile they were looking for. I was entirely unaware that I was that sort of person!

I was a Baptist by conviction, and I had definite views on why I considered the Baptists as the preferable choice among the denominations. The Baptist Union of Great Britain has three

Declarations of Principles by which it is constituted, and it does not use creeds as a requirement of membership in the way other denominations do. Part of the first Declaration is that 'each church has the liberty, under the guidance of the Holy Spirit, to interpret and administer His [*Jesus*'] Laws', and this appealed to my understanding of how believers should be able to operate together in a church setting. One of the weaknesses of this viewpoint, however, is that there is little or even no regard for the value of other forms of churchmanship. Ecumenism had thus had a low priority for me up to this point. After all, I had made an objective choice to be a Baptist, and its forms of government and worship were more than sufficient to meet my needs. Why would I want to abandon such long-held principles?

Nonetheless, to honour John's confidence in me, I agreed to be interviewed by St Thomas's appointments team, but I have to admit to a distinct lack of enthusiasm. There were several immediate reasons why I thought there would be difficulties with such a position – for a start, I was non-liturgical and did not like robes; the church was also part of the 'establishment'; and what if they raised their funds through whist drives? There was also, of course, the thorny issue of baptism. In hindsight it amazes me how ungracious I must have appeared to the appointments team and to others at St Thomas's, and I have several times felt the need to repent of this unfair caricature of Anglicans.

Twenty minutes into the interview, I realised that they were serious about this appointment – and, what's more, I needed to adopt a similar position and a greater degree of humility. At that point I knew God was calling me to be part of the team at this very exciting church. The rest, as the saying goes, is history.

The paradigm shift in both theology and practice which I have described was not a reaction against sterile conservative evangelicalism, which has many strengths. It was, rather, part of my continuing journey in search of authenticity, which I firmly believe is rooted in the integrity of the gospel message. The shift in my theology became the means of relinquishing the legalism of the spiritual straitjacket which I had cultivated over many years. I began to move into a deeper experiential aspect of what I now believe it means to be in Christ and part of his kingdom.

Objectively I always subscribed to the belief that Christ was present every time people gathered in his name. Subjectively I rarely experienced it, because my conditioning and background told me that good biblical exposition was preferable to allowing my emotions and inner spirit to engage. Feelings were not to be trusted. It was important to be in control, to keep a stiff upper lip in matters of spiritual experience. After all, God was 'a gentleman' who would surely never embarrass us with signs of apparent weakness such as weeping, laughing and releasing worshippers to move and dance in response to his presence, much less enrich our ministry with such 'additions'.

Since embarking on the new path, I have personally experienced, and have observed in the lives of others, the healing of inner hurts through the power of the Holy Spirit. I have also seen physical healing, once most memorably during a trip to Nepal to visit churches in the Gorkha region with a Nepalese pastor we support. We were required to use a trekking agency in order to enter the area, and the leader of the agency was a Christian who employed believers as well as Hindus. One day during the trek the porters were at least half an hour ahead of the main party and one of the Hindus was stung on the finger by a scorpion. By the time we caught up with him his hand had swollen to nearly twice its normal size. We had no medical supplies for such an emergency, so we offered to pray for him in the name of Jesus. He consented and, as we prayed, the swelling stopped and he was greatly relieved. By the following morning his hand had returned to its normal size. Much discussion ensued among the porters, and Mosa, our Nepalese pastor, explained about Jesus' power to heal. After the third day the healed porter agreed to become a Christian, and he invited Mosa to visit his family and his village to tell them about Jesus.

As well as many other occasions of healing, I have witnessed the effects of demonisation melt away through the invocation of the name of Jesus, and have seen people released from their bondage. The longer I am involved in ministry, the more I am convinced that the kingdom of God is a reality, evidenced by the demonstration of his power and involving much more than a mere intellectual response to some creed or confession of faith.

Application to the wider church

It is interesting to note that in the UK, where there is a major decline in church membership and attendance, the churches which have adopted the methodology and theology of VMI have experienced significant growth at all levels. Holy Trinity, Brompton, St Andrew's, Chorleywood and St Thomas's, Sheffield all have congregations of more than 1,500. They also all have semi-formal networks of churches which have, for the most part, healthy and growing congregations. In the Baptist Union those churches which are growing use a similar methodology, as do churches associated with the Ichthus Fellowship in London headed by Roger Forster, and New Frontiers International led by Terry Virgo. The New Wine annual gathering in August attracts in excess of 30,000 participants representing over 400 churches, and is unashamedly committed to VMI values.

This reflects the narrative of the Acts of the Apostles, which presents a community who were unified and bold in their prayer, and who, notably, prayed not primarily for others but for themselves. In Acts 4:24–31 we read that the believers prayed for courage and power in their witness, and as a consequence 'they were all filled with the Holy Spirit and spoke the word of God boldly' (v. 31). The writer, Luke, presents the empowerment of the Holy Spirit as the main influence and force behind the effective mission of the early church. It is my firm belief that the church needs to recover the same impact of the Holy Spirit's ministry today.

The early Christians, severely persecuted and fleeing for their lives (Acts 8), sought to spread the gospel in spite of their suffering, and apparently overcame all manner of obstacles in helping the church to grow at a phenomenal rate. Michael Green calls these people informal missionaries who used every opportunity at their disposal to spread the good news. He comments:

> This must often have been not formal preaching, but the informal chattering to friends and chance acquaintances, in homes and wine shops, on walks, and around market stalls. They went everywhere gossiping the gospel; they did it naturally, enthusiastically, and with the conviction of those who are not paid to say that sort of thing.[4]

---

[4] Michael Green, *Evangelism in the Early Church* (Kingsway, 2003).

Clearly the gospel and the changes it brought into the lives of these early believers affected them to such an extent that they were able to overcome the cultural difficulties of their time. An example of this can be seen in Acts 17 where Paul, while waiting for Silas and Timothy to join him in Athens, cannot escape the plethora of idols in the city. The text suggests that he did not allow this encounter with the trappings of pagan Athenian culture to deter him in his aim to spread the gospel – indeed, he moved into the marketplace to take a closer look at the inscriptions on the images. This resulted in a debate with the leaders of the Athenian society at the Areopagus, the centre for philosophical discussion. Adopting the approach of a cultural anthropologist, Paul was able to debate intelligently with them about Jesus and his kingdom and the many gods they worshipped. His theology allowed for the possibility that God was at work everywhere, even amidst this idolatrous culture.

Studying the imperatives which motivated those in the early church helped St Thomas's to see that the dry tradition and mechanical emulation of the modern church needed to be changed. The ills of the current church situation could only be addressed by going right back to the beginning and studying the way in which the original, dynamic church was depicted in Acts.

It is obvious that in the Western church there is a virus in the body which has contributed to its rate of decline, a rate not considered possible 60 years ago. A lack of nerve about the gospel and its power is reflected in the lives of the people who make up its membership. Many plans and schemes have been offered to help reverse the decline, but except in isolated pockets they have largely been unsuccessful. Clarity about the church's function, ministry and worship patterns which served previous generations well no longer seems to be relevant or effective to the current and emerging generations. With such a prognosis, and from a worldly perspective, the simple passage of time inevitably means that the church, as it has been known, will cease to exist.

Today, in order to cope with the pressures and difficulties of life, the world turns to psychologists, personal coaches and self-help books, seeking always to lay hold of that ever-elusive feeling of peace. The church, in addressing its own ills, has begun to use similar sources in the hope that a solution will be found. Colin Williams' comment rightly summarises the issue: 'The swaddling clothes of metaphysics – of thinking from above by dependence on outside principles – have been cast off.'[5] Instead of looking at biblical principles and the God who lies behind them, and reading the text for what it says, the church has superimposed an empirical, open, functional and technocratic model – largely because the Scriptures seem to lack credibility in today's world. The result is a religion which has more to do with a controlled and superficial life than with the dynamic, living faith Jesus intended it to be. Jesus, as Lord of the church possessing all authority in heaven and earth, declared, 'I will build my church and the gates of hell will not overcome it' (Matthew 16:18).

The following chapters contain a critique of this super-imposed model of Christendom, and I shall seek to address, humbly and sensitively, the restrictions such a model has placed on the mission of the church. Institutions, for the most part, operate in a survival mode, and until recently the church has had a degree of success in maintaining its tradition and rich heritage. The time has come, however, to abandon the survival

---

[5] Colin Williams, *Faith in a Secular Age* (Collins, 1966), p. 42.

mode, to sacrifice those aspects of tradition which are in conflict with the church's *raison d'être*, and to come to terms with the implications of intoning, 'Your kingdom come, your will be done on earth as in heaven . . .'

Since I am a Baptist by persuasion rather than upbringing, and a convert is generally more certain about what and why he believes, I tend to reflect a more dogmatic approach to theology and how it applies to ecclesiology. I hope, therefore, that my approach will be seen to be pragmatic in the best sense of the word, and my explorations presented with fairness and integrity. The methodology and principles which I shall outline could be criticised as being yet another discipleship programme, or even just a trendy way of doing church by pandering to the culture and spirit of the age. I ask you to look beyond this perspective and to judge by the fruit of the outworking of these principles at St Thomas's Church, where I have the privilege to serve.

3

Mission to Builders, Boomers and Busters

Living in a postmodern society which is also post-denomina-tional and post-Christian means that newcomers to the church have few reference points to help them engage with what goes on in the average church. The text on a website called 'thething todo.com' created by a member of St Thomas's helps to illus-trate the increasing gulf that exists between the emerging gen-eration and the church. It reads as follows:

We're a bunch of people in the Sheffield ghettos who are living com-munity – supporting each other thru all the bad stuff that's going down. In love with Jesus, but wanting to get away from all the baggage of institutionalised 'church' (though we still love it, of course – they're our spiritual mummies & daddies & keep us in check). We've seen plenty of expressions of 'nu church' jump into the arena – internet communities etc – but they've mostly all faded away, leaving us with nothing other than just a desire to be with the big G & do the greater things that he promised, because that sounds like fun & he's much much nicer than Western thinking tells us he is. So we've set up this lovely site to easily keep in touch with each other & see if anyone fancies praying or seeing what club/gig God's gone to that night or whatever – to be spontaneous & organic & other exciting sounding buzz words, because having a regular 'service' would be just too boring. Amennnnn.

At St Thomas's we seek to be faithful to our respective traditions whenever possible. While we do not wear robes at our celebration events, at an Anglican confirmation the ordained staff members wear their dog collars and the bishop usually wears his mitre and alb, and sometimes a cope, and carries his crozier. His chaplain and archdeacon generally accompany him. The intention is to make the occasion a grand and memorable one for the candidates, and to indicate that we are part of the wider church. Those unaccustomed to such pomp nonetheless recognise this as a memorable and meaningful way of publicly demonstrating one's faith in Christ, and often people say, 'I would like to do that too.' When St Thomas's shows its complementary Baptist dimension and holds a believer's baptism, employing all the drama of that occasion, the same folk often say they want to do that as well. When we explain that there is a theological difference between the acts of confirmation and believer's baptism, they struggle with the choice, because they do not have a grid of reference that resonates with the worldview of denominationalism. It is not that they do not want to make a public confession of their faith, but rather that they have difficulty with the concept of deciding whether to take on the label of either 'Anglican' or 'Baptist'. The postmodern generation has a natural suspicion of institutions, of which the church is just one among many.

I recognise that this creates problems for many church

leaders, for whom such matters are essential for good order and accountability, as well as being important in terms of church tradition. Yet if it is to be effective in mission to the postmodern world, the church has to re-examine what enables effective mission to happen. Cultural setting is an important part of this process, and Mike Breen's insight has been a vital factor at St Thomas's in targeting specific people groups which the church traditionally has been unable to reach. He has a remarkable ability to observe life, to understand the emerging generation and to assess the influences which drive the spirit of the age. His input and vision have resulted in a fair degree of success for St Thomas's in reaching out to a high proportion of people under the age of 40.

Generally, the church has been slow to recognise the importance of understanding this dimension of mission. The irony is that those being prepared for work overseas spend a lot of time researching the culture of the country or region in which they are to serve. Their preparation includes study of the language, protocol, geography and rites of passage of the destination country, in order that they may plan how to make the gospel relevant. Thanks to immigration, secularism and the effects of postmodernism, all countries in the developed world, including the UK, are just as complex as those countries where missionaries traditionally work, yet the church somehow remains blissfully ignorant of the issues it faces at home.

Cultural statistics

Ninety years ago in the UK, the church was more certain of its influence in society than it is today, and in the last 40 years membership has declined at an alarming rate. Between 1980

and 1990 the Church of England lost 1,000 adherents a week –
800 of whom were under the age of 30. The most recent census
indicates that in spite of concerted efforts such as the Decade
of Evangelism, launched in 1990, attendance has now declined
to a level where an average of 2,200 people a week are leaving
the church.[1] The greatest loss has been among those under 19
years of age. Other traditional denominations are experiencing
decline on a similar scale.

The church has traditionally acted as the guardian of the
nation's morals, as well as being a pillar of stability for family
and public life. The fact that the House of Lords has bishops
sitting on its benches indicates the position they allegedly hold
in the government of the country. However, their influence
seems to carry little weight in the lives of the general populace.
Decline in church membership and general loss of influence has
brought inevitable consequences. Every day in Britain at least
480 couples are divorced, and the number of children born to
teenage mothers is the highest in Europe.[2] In a 1978 study of
the USA Robert Wuthnow demonstrated that, out of those
born between 1944 and 1960, nearly half were single or
divorced; more than two thirds had changed residence in the
previous five years; two thirds had stopped participating in
religious organisations, and only 13 per cent attended church or
synagogue weekly.[3] Such statistics indicate that institutional
churches are not making much headway at a moral or evangelistic level on either side of the Atlantic.

---

[1] Peter Brierley, *The Tide Is Running Out* (Christian Research, 2000), p. 129.

[2] Cited in *Alpha News*, March 1996, p. 9.

[3] Robert Wuthnow, *After Heaven: Spirituality in America since the 1950s*
(University of California Press, 1998), p. 75.

The Builder generation (those born before 1945) form the bulk of current church membership in the UK, and as will be seen later in this chapter they have little hope of attracting either Boomers (those born between 1946 and 1964) or Generation X, also known as Busters (those born between 1965 and 1985). Small numbers in churches, the increasing age gap and an inability to relate meaningfully to the current prevailing culture all militate against winning many of the younger generation into the kingdom of God by using a methodology pertinent to their early years in the church. It is simply not happening. Many of those currently in leadership are in their late fifties or early sixties, and they tend to see themselves as the 'guardians' of church tradition: they, after all, are generally the people responsible for administering denominational affairs. For the most part, therefore, the church has stayed 'old' and is almost unable to adapt and be relevant to the culture of the day. Leaving aside for a moment the question of Generation X, Boomers in the UK have largely rejected the faith of their parents, the Builders, and there are no indications that they will return to the traditional denominational churches.

While there are aspects of any culture that the gospel opposes, Steve Scott rightly comments in his book, *Like a House on Fire: Renewal in Postmodern Culture*, 'We must remember that we are *within* culture, and our calling in Christ is to play our part in the redemption and transformation of individuals and cultures.'[4] This does not mean that importing hi-tech equipment, flashing lights and contemporary music will resolve the issue. It means that understanding the needs of the

---

[4] Steve Scott, *Like a House on Fire* (Cornerstone, 1997), p. 46.

prevailing culture is a vital step towards demonstrating that the gospel has a better way of answering those needs, which in turn should be evident in the life of those who make up the church.

The emerging generation, with its ideological relativism, has a tolerance that validates any form of spirituality and is not conducive to traditional forms of evangelism. Members of this generation do not share the faith 'once delivered', nor do they share the collective memories and assumptions of the Christian faith, nor do they understand its vocabulary. To speak of Jesus as being 'the way, the truth and the life, which leads to the Father' is too dogmatic for a culture that sees many paths to God. That is why it is so important that we understand the world to which the church is called to proclaim the gospel. If we do not know who we are talking to, how can we communicate effectively?

A confused social order

I am privileged to conduct many weddings at St Thomas's. As part of the ceremony I ask both sets of parents if they will accept, honour and respect their new son- or daughter-in-law as part of their extended family. This public declaration is a helpful way of determining that the couple being married have the blessing of their parents, as well as emphasising that they are 'leaving their father and mother' to set up their own unit as husband and wife. Reflecting the national statistics, a high proportion of the couples' parents are divorced. While there is often some embarrassment when divorced parents are asked to stand to give their assent, in the main it works out all right. On one occasion, however, we decided to forgo this part of the ceremony, because the bridegroom's parents had been divorced and remarried three times, and *all* the partners were attending the service!

The rising rate of divorce, particularly for Boomers, the parents of the emerging generation, is one of the factors that has threatened the nuclear family. Single-parent family units and co-habiting couples are on the increase, and it is predicted married couples will fall from 64% in 1981 to 38% by 2021.[5] Divorce has become a monument to personal failure, a symbol of broken dreams, and a breakdown in the basic component of community. In its wake, self-doubt and self-recrimination have led to a confused social order, which has compounded society's inability to relate in the meaningful way God intended for his creation. In this painfully fragmented situation there are so many needs to be met that it is difficult for most people to believe there is a loving God who cares for them. How can they imagine such a God when they experience so little care and love from those – a husband, a wife, a parent – from whom they have a right to expect it?

The first question in the Shorter Westminster Catechism asks, 'What is the chief end of man?' The answer, 'Man's chief end is to glorify God and enjoy him for ever', indicates that it is meant to be a dynamic relationship. Thomas Vincent's seventeenth-century commentary, *The Shorter Catechism Explained from Scripture*, says that this action of glorifying God should happen 'because he hath made them, and made them for this end, and given them a soul capable of doing it beyond rational creatures'. This dynamic aspect is the missing dimension in the church's witness concerning our relationship with God, and even the dialogue of prayer seems moribund in comparison with what it is intended to be.

---

[5] 'Family Life' in *Quadrant* (July, 2000), p. 3.

Leonard Sweet encapsulates what should be happening in this unique relationship, for which the church has been entrusted to win every generation, whether modern or postmodern:

> Prayer is attuning our beings to the frequencies of the Spirit until 'resonance' with the divine is reached. When we reach those full registers where mysterious things happen, then something has to give, and our lives are transformed, transfigured, if you will, into the divine image.[6]

Part of the failure of the traditional church is that it has become syncretistic and has not declared the uniqueness of Jesus Christ. Instead of confronting the world with its clear gospel message, it has blended into the surrounding culture, becoming indistinct. An example of this appeared in *The Times* newspaper:

> A survey by the Cost of Conscience pressure group seems to imply that many of the pulpits of the Church of England are filled with closet atheists. According to its recent survey of some 2,000 clergy, only three in ten women priests and six in ten male priests believe in the Virgin Birth; only half of women priests and seven in ten male priests believe in the physical Resurrection of Christ. Here they stand – not actually believing 75 per cent of what they preach each Sunday.[7]

What is more, the church seems unable to grapple with the cultural impact of globalisation and the changes that has brought

---

[6] Leonard Sweet, *Faithquake* (Abingdon, 1994), p. 62.

[7] Nicholas Henderson, 'You better believe it (but we don't)', *The Times*, 1st August 2002, Section 2, p. 2.

at all levels, particularly with relevance to the emerging generation. Because resonance with an almighty and holy God is absent in the church, and the mysterious effect of the presence and power of the Holy Spirit is not expected, the church seems to have become irrelevant.

The Boomers

The 1960s were the adolescent years of the Boomers, the parents of the current emerging generation. This decade aggravated an already over-developed sense of entitlement, producing a narcissistic generation that deified individualism. As youngsters they had lived under the curtailment of wartime restrictions and, understandably, when they became parents they did not want their offspring to suffer the same privations.

The churches to which the Boomer generation was exposed represented an order formed by leadership and scholarship – an order which Archbishop William Temple accurately described as formed by 'men who spent blameless lives giving entirely orthodox answers to questions no one was asking'.[8] Maintaining tradition and the status quo and upholding its attendant bureaucracy was considered to be of greater importance than proclaiming the life-changing message of the gospel. Tradition is undeniably important; it is essential that it should be rehearsed and told in ways that give form and meaning to a community's past and offer continuity into the future. Church tradition, when properly conveyed, is evidence of a living faith, but when it degenerates into traditionalism, it is merely portraying the dead faith of those who are alive at the time.

---

[8] David Watson, *I Believe in Evangelism* (Eerdmans, 1976), p. 14.

The church failed to demonstrate and communicate the gospel's life-changing message to the Boomer generation, and in its failure it created a deep-seated cynicism towards formalised religion. Boomers left the church in droves on reaching the age of discretion. They were still spiritual beings, but their emerging counterculture leaned towards an exploration of the perceived 'larger mysteries' of the universe, particularly through Eastern religions. Christianity became increasingly marginalised.

Relationships also underwent redefinition, and increasingly the standard family unit characteristic of the Boomers' parents was abandoned. Divorce and same-sex relationships became more common. The introduction of the contraceptive pill compounded the situation and many took to a lifestyle of promiscuity, which ultimately resulted in an epidemic of sexually transmitted diseases, the most deadly being AIDS. Boomers accepted anything that would further their hedonistic lifestyle. Long working hours, a cut-throat drive for professional advancement and more income, and dual careers for couples, whether married or not, became necessary to support a voracious appetite for travel and possessions. By the 1980s, the abandonment of the Judaeo–Christian values which had played a significant part in previous generations had led to a worldview which perceived greed as a virtue. Social scientists define this generation as the last to have been influenced by Enlightenment education and thought processes.

The problems of Generation X

The offspring of the Boomers, known as Busters or Xers, see themselves as victims of the excesses of their parents. The lifestyle modelled for them had no boundaries or good examples of rules for living. They are the first postmodern generation.

The sexual revolution of their parents, with contraception and abortion on demand, has reinforced the feeling that they were not wanted: many are not sure they were wanted as children, seeing themselves as accidents or escapees of the contraceptive pill. Many were reared in nurseries while their parents worked, confirming a sense of alienation from the basic unit of the family community. When they were at home, television was often the only means of information-gathering and comfort, and it even acted as a surrogate parent.

Blended families (that is, those where the parents had been divorced and remarried, bringing children from previous relationships), while at least giving some community integration, further distorted the concept of marriage and provided poor models of family life. The fact that many parents – whether married, unmarried or of the same sex – pursued dual careers resulted in a generation of latchkey kids who never had a childhood and who, for the most part, raised themselves. High divorce rates created many single-parent families in which the parent had to work out of economic necessity, compounding further the deprivation felt by the children. They no longer expect to be taken care of – instead, a streetwise pragmatism tells them that if they are to survive, they must make it on their own. Moreover, Boomers at least started off with a concept that sexual promiscuity was wrong, but they never conveyed that to their children, because by then they had adapted it into their lifestyle. Their children, the Busters, faced with such a model, do not perceive promiscuity as a taboo. A young girl who was converted through St Thomas's after coming up to university in the city admitted that one of the things she had looked forward to prior to conversion was getting as much sex as possible. Her broken family background meant that this was a form of intimacy she craved.

Members of Generation X also have little expectation that education will produce the necessary qualifications that will lead to meaningful and lasting jobs.[9] They believe that the Boomers have snatched all the good jobs, with their attendant security – and that in the process they have lost their souls. For evidence, Busters point to the world they have inherited, with its massive economic problems and an environment sacrificed on the altar of prestigious cars, aerosols and indiscriminate burning of fossil fuels. High unemployment has further reduced the quality of life that lies before them.

Another problem for Xers is information overload – thanks to the kind of education they have received and the grid through which modern life is processed. Some would say that they are creative because they grew up with TV, video games, movies and computers, and are always on the lookout for that which is fresh, creative and new. In consequence they feel they are not bound to the past, but seek to develop their own solutions for any problems, old or new. They choose to live by whatever rules are necessary for survival, because the problems of the world and the difficulties of their lives are too complex to resolve. They pursue whatever path gives relief, and this has produced a variety of worldviews with varying degrees of validity – a philosophy for which there is no core of absolute truth. Celia Brayfield describes their minimalist approach to life:

> They don't do belief, they just do spiritual, which seldom goes farther than a Feng Shui phrase. They don't do love, or friendship,

---

[9] Richard Peace, 'Living in the Shadow of the Baby Boomers', paper for the Consultation on Reaching Baby Busters, Leighton Ford Ministries and InterVarsity Christian Fellowship, 27th–28th October 1993, p. 2.

or sentimentality. They always have reasons not to do commitment at this point in time and mostly they don't do people at all.[10]

Celia Brayfield's comments underline a missing dimension in the upbringing of this generation. We were never created to be alone, and there is a natural hunger for love and community that needs to be satisfied. Unfortunately, the model of their parents was not a good one and Xers harbour a natural suspicion against using them as examples of stable and meaningful relationships. However, when an authentic model that has integrity and works well is demonstrated and attracts their peers, natural curiosity begs investigation. What is it about, and is it worth pursuing? It is my belief that the redeeming effect of the gospel is the only option and needs to be possessed at any cost. This is the only way we can change the brokenness that is the lot of humankind. But how do we communicate this healing news to a lost generation?

Conflict of priorities

The fragmentation of society has left people with a hunger for a solution that will overcome loneliness, emptiness and the dysfunction they see all around them. We are meant for community – we need to relate to each other, to share common experiences, to be affirmed, to receive advice and friendship. Part of society's response to the lack of community has been to create a plethora of self-help groups. *Newsweek* reports that in any given week in the USA, 15 million people attend half a

---

[10] Celia Brayfield, 'Generation Bland', *The Times*, 7th August 2000, Section 2, p. 3.

million support groups for their afflictions and addictions. This indicates both a hunger in the soul and a real desire to resolve the dilemma.[11] Martin Seligman, however, comments on how such 'self-help' solutions are bound to fail:

> Surely one necessary (although hardly sufficient) condition for finding meaning in our lives is an attachment to something larger than the lonely self. To the extent that young people now find it hard to take seriously their relationship with God, to care about their relationship with the country or to be part of a large abiding family, they will find it very difficult to find. To put it another way, the self is a very poor site for finding meaning in life.[12]

Society on both sides of the Atlantic has become increasingly secularised, post-Christian and, in the UK in particular, post-denominational. Nonetheless, since all are created in the image of God, the longing for the spiritual in the human soul is still there and needs to be satisfied. God is there, he is not silent, and he can be found, if the declaration that Jesus made is correct: 'I am the way and the truth and the life. No one comes to the Father except through me' (John 14:6). Currently, however, the search is not concentrated on Christ alone, but takes place against the backdrop of a confused world where there are no reliable reference points. George Hunter's assessment of the challenge to the church is correct: 'Most of our neighbours do not share our faith, or our assumptions, or our vocabulary. The West is once again a vast mission field.'[13]

---

[11] Darius Salter, *American Evangelism: Its Theory and Practice* (Baker, 1996), p. 196.

[12] Martin E.P. Seligman, 'Boomers', *Psychology Today*.

[13] George Hunter, *How to Reach Secular People* (Abingdon, 1992), p. 37.

The widespread impact of Eastern religions further complicates the church's problem in witnessing to the current scene. Relatively cheap travel to formerly remote countries has created a global village, which in turn has given access and a higher profile to other cultures and religions. The failure of traditional church denominations to offer an attractive alternative to these influences has led many to seek spiritual fulfilment through means other than Christianity. These alternative paths often appear more exciting because they are mystical and other-worldly, and not as ominous or prescriptive as the heavily structured denominational churches of the West. The postmodern generation's tendency is to search for a style that makes little demand for serious change in their lives, and Eastern religions certainly seem more attractive in this regard. In his book *Inside the Mind of Unchurched Harry and Mary*, Lee Strobel speaks of this trait: 'Whilst Harry might be willing to sign up for a cause, he's less likely to sign up with an institution. There's an aversion – again, mostly among younger people – to formally joining anything.'[14]

It is imperative that the church should become relevant to this lost and confused generation, and that it should be able to communicate the powerful alternative which Christ offers. How can we cross that huge gulf in understanding and outlook? One might say that Don Richardson faced a similarly challenging experience in the early 1960s, when he went to work with the headhunting and cannibal Sawi tribe in New Guinea. Their culture applauded treachery as a way of life, to such an extent that they would 'fatten with friendship' any guests from other

---

[14] Lee Strobel, *Inside the Mind of Unchurched Harry and Mary* (Zondervan, 1993), p. 71.

tribes, in order that they might become victims for slaughter. They would then feast on the flesh and 'capture the spirit' of the victim. Richardson describes his first meeting with this tribe in the following way:

> A meeting with culturally similar strangers is one thing, but a meeting of culturally dissimilar strangers is something else! Representing opposite ends of humanity's wide-ranging cultural spectrum, we faced each other, and the very air between us seemed to crackle with tension.[15]

Richardson's tale of his encounter with the Sawi tribe expresses the same extreme wariness with which most church members view the postmodern generation. Tension, mistrust and a complete polarisation of attitude prevail. Even though the two generations are related, and even though they live in the same society, they are as culturally apart as Christians and cannibals. At St Thomas's one day, in a discussion with one of our Builder/Boomer members, a Generation Xer asked if it would be all right to smoke pot during a worship session. Without batting an eyelid, and demonstrating the insight he had into the culture from which the young questioner came, the older man answered wisely, 'If the effect of the Holy Spirit runs out, feel free!'

---

[15] Don Richardson, *Peace Child* (G/L Publications, 1974), p. 116.

4

Church Order in the New Testament

A biblical baseline

Like most churches, St Thomas's seeks to participate in the general mission of God. We work alongside all the other ministries of the universal church, yet at the same time seek to be obedient to the specific expression of this mission with regard to our community and city, through the vision and gifts of those who make up our membership. In order to harness the energy of the large number of young people who worship with us, we have found that it is important to seek intentionally to identify, train and disciple them to that end. Individualism is an icon of modern culture, but the New Testament shows that the early church was at its most effective when it operated as a community. The book of Acts has been particularly helpful to us in this regard.

Three phases can be identified in the life of the early church community in the narrative of Acts, and these gave the leadership at St Thomas's a format from which to establish the church's ministry and mission policy. Each phase shows characteristics that resulted in growth and increased influence for the early church. The narrative begins with Jesus, just before he ascended into heaven, telling the disciples, 'You will receive power when the Holy Spirit comes on you; and you will be my witnesses in Jerusalem, and in all Judea and Samaria, and to the ends of the earth' (Acts 1:8). By this he indicated that their ministry and mission would take them well beyond their geographical boundaries, and that they would possess the same power by which his own earthly ministry had operated.

The first phase started on the Day of Pentecost. Peter, empowered by the Holy Spirit, preached to the crowds and 3,000 converts were added to the embryonic church. Life in the new community of believers was consolidated through the teaching of the apostles under the strong leadership of Peter, and later James, the Lord's brother (Acts 2:42–47). Clear evidence that the message and work of the church was authentic and life-changing is shown in the large numbers being added daily to the membership (v. 47). So strong was the sense of community that it is recorded, 'There were no needy persons among them' (Acts 4:34). They were also 'highly regarded by the people' in Jerusalem (Acts 5:13). The number of men in the church soon reached 5,000 (Acts 4:4), then more men and women were added (Acts 5:14). As a result, 'The word of God spread. The number of disciples increased rapidly' (Acts 6:7). This kingdom equation of increase through preaching and spreading the word through the witness of believers and consolidation through teaching enabled the new disciples to see the church being steadily multiplied. Inevitably, however, the church's influence created difficulties for the governing authorities and resulted in persecution (Acts 8:4). Many of the believers were scattered because of this persecution.

The second phase followed a similar pattern. The anointed preaching of Philip in Samaria (Acts 8:5) was accompanied by signs of the power of the Holy Spirit, bringing similar miraculous events to those seen in Jerusalem. The crowds who heard the message of the gospel believed and were baptised (Acts 8:6, 12). Later the message was consolidated by the planting of churches in Judea, Galilee and Samaria and, as they grew stronger, so they multiplied (Acts 9:31). Persecution followed, just as it had done in Jerusalem (Acts 11:19, 20), but this was followed by the positive process of consolidation in Antioch. Such was the rate of expansion that the mother church in Jerusalem sent Barnabas to verify the extent of the growth (Acts 11:22–24). By this stage the early church was clearly fulfilling Jesus' promise that they would be his witnesses in Jerusalem, Judea and Samaria, and they were beginning to see evidence that they were going out to the ends of the earth.

The third phase began at Ephesus and once again used the same pattern, detailed in Acts 19. Growth was always the outcome when centres such as Jerusalem, Antioch and Ephesus were consolidated under strong leadership and biblical teaching and rooted in the anointing of the Holy Spirit. Peter, followed by James, led the church in Jerusalem. Philip did the same in Samaria, and Paul in Ephesus, succeeded by the apostle John. Ephesus became the centre of influence for the wider church for the next 400 years.

It was from this perspective that Mike Breen deduced how the 'Ephesus' model should be used at St Thomas's – so that the church might increase, spread and multiply, in confirmation of the word he had received before taking up his responsibilities as leader. Part of the preparation for this process involved a reconsideration of the central biblical passages relating to the person and work of the Holy Spirit (Romans 12; 1 Corinthians 12; Ephesians 4), on the basis that the gifts and offices present in the early church are still operative and normative for today. Without such empowerment, the church would be unable to grow in the way it was designed. Romans 12 offered us insight into how the church should function, and 1 Corinthians 12 showed us how the Holy Spirit manifested his presence when people gathered together or worshipped. The traditional Christendom interpretation of Ephesians 4 cites apostles, prophets, evangelists, pastors and teachers as being the leaders in the church. As I shall explain, however, Mike Breen's reasoning from the text was that these gifts are given to the members of the church *as a whole*, regardless of status, gender or authority, thus enabling all members to be a true expression of God's missionary people. This text has become a major factor in equipping St Thomas's members for its mission.

Romans 12: functional gifts of the Holy Spirit

The epistles to the Corinthians and the Romans were both written to specific church settings, whereas scholars on the whole agree that Ephesians was written as a more general letter to the churches at large. The letter to the Romans was probably written from Greece (Acts 20:2) as Paul was preparing to go to Jerusalem (Romans 15:25) with the money he had collected for the saints (Galatians 2:10; 1 Corinthians 16:1–4; 2 Corinthians 8–9). Near the end of the epistle (Romans 15:22–24) he is more specific about his plans for a western mission to Spain, which he hopes will be served by the resources of the Roman believers. The letter is rightly interpreted by many scholars as a handbook of Christian doctrine, but it also includes Paul's distilled wisdom, summed up in his missionary theology and experience, and gives insight into what the church should be engaged in with regard to mission.

Romans 12 briefly echoes 1 Corinthians 12–14 on ministries and love and speaks about the 'living sacrifices' required of believers when they give themselves completely to God (Romans 12:1). The word translated 'serve' or 'offer' indicates not a mere isolated event, but a continuous action, a process, chosen by the believer as a result of his or her surrender to the will of God. The imperative 'therefore', followed by logical argument, supports and explains what Christ has already done and calls all believers to the service of God with renewed minds, given by the Holy Spirit. With those renewed minds, they are able to determine what pleases God. The church, the body comprising the believing community, is the environment in which the effects of God's Spirit on all their faculties function at the optimum level. This only comes about when all is given to God and put under his sovereignty and will. Dunn rightly comments, 'Paul uses the body of Christ as an ecclesiological concept only in connection with charisms. The Christian community exists for him as a *charismatic community*,' that is, a community that uses the gifts of the Holy Spirit God gives to the church.[1] It is not human endeavour that creates this, but the work of the Holy Spirit on the human spirit.

Paul lists seven ways of serving the church through the manifestation of God's grace as empowered by the Holy Spirit (Romans 12:6–8). The first four reflect the outworking of those in the community who are gathered for worship – namely,

---

[1] James D.G. Dunn, *Word Biblical Commentary, Vol. 38, Romans 9–16* (Word Publishers, 1988), p. 723, italics mine.

prophesying, serving, teaching and encouraging. The last three show how the function of the church can be further complemented through giving, exercising leadership and demonstrating mercy. Eugene Peterson's paraphrase is a good amplification of what Paul seeks to convey: 'Each of us finds our function as part of the body . . . so since we find ourselves fashioned into all these excellently formed and marvellously functioning parts in Christ's body, let's just go ahead and be what we are made to be.'[2] In other words, let the church function as a community. An important point to note is that Paul describes the particular types or manifestations of the grace God gives to each member (Romans 12:6), not the *degree* of that grace. The key to Paul's argument here is the word 'function' (v. 4), and this corresponds with Peter's exhortation, 'Each one should use whatever gift he has received to serve others, faithfully administrating God's grace in its various forms' (1 Peter 4:10).

Paul urges the Roman believers to see that they are firmly linked to one another as a community – something quite different from any other unity they might have experienced before, or were likely to encounter outside the sphere of the church. If God has anointed and called a person into membership of his church, then it is logical that a choice, an act of volition, is required as to whether they exercise the grace given to them by Christ in that community. Hence his exhortation in verse 6, 'We have [literally *having*] different gifts, according to the grace given us', is only effective when used in the unique personal and corporate way that God has designed.

Paul goes on to describe how these expressions of grace are demonstrated in the actions of church members, by using the

---

[2] Eugene H. Peterson, *The Message* (Navpress, 1993), p. 328.

participles *prohistamenous* (administrating or leading), functioning alongside *didaskón* (teaching), *parakalõn* (exhorting) and *eleõn* (doing acts of mercy). He does not explain exactly *why* they have to function like this, but seems to be describing the normative practice in the churches he planted during his missionary journeys. The same could be said of his description of the fivefold ministries in Ephesians 4, where he does not mention the qualifications of those involved as if they were officials within the church, but prefaces each section by indicating that *each one of you* functions and participates in these ways.

In the modern church, these functions could be described as the responsibilities of leaders, pastors and teachers, or those who welcome members and visitors, and those who are of a pastoral disposition, who exercise grace and mercy, and enable the work of the church to be effective. Paul's description, however, is of a body of people who, by the fusion of grace imparted to them as believers, understand that God's will and purpose reflects the relationship they have with him (UP), which is manifested by their relationship to each other (IN) and, in turn, is offered to the community in which they live and serve (OUT). Each member has a distinct contribution or function, and draws on the grace of God to become an example of a 'living sacrifice'.

The desire of St Thomas's Church, under the leadership of Mike Breen, is to emulate these qualities as imparted by the Holy Spirit and described by Paul. To have a church that functioned in this way would be such a powerful and effective ministry, not only to its members, but also to a wider public. Such a community would be able to serve other churches in the region, as well as in the rest of the country and overseas, because it would have no other option than to operate as the Lord of the church desires. To this end, the Lifeskills course has become part of the mechanism by which members are helped to understand and identify their part and function in the church.

1 Corinthians 12: gifts in the context of the gathered people of God

Like Romans, 1 Corinthians was written to a specific church situation. It is actually the third in a series of exchanges between Paul and the church in Corinth (1 Corinthians 5:9; 7:1), and he seeks to address issues which had impaired the effectiveness of their ministry. His aim is to convince them that his reasoning, as the founding apostle, is God's perspective, and that they are in error on these particular issues. The letter is designed to help them recognise the true nature of the life of the Spirit in their community, so that they can grow in maturity and extend the kingdom of God in Corinth. The issue of worship (1 Corinthians 11–14) and the advice Paul gives about the manifestation of the gifts of the Holy Spirit have had a particular bearing on the theological foundations of the worship life at St Thomas's, and on the subject matter of this book.

A popular interpretation of the list of gifts in 1 Corinthians 12 is simply to add them to the lists in Romans 12 and Ephesians 4. Bruce Bugbee, who heads up Network Ministries International and was part of Willow Creek Church in Chicago, follows other commentators who categorise the gifts of 1 Corinthians in this way: 'The most extensive New Testament passage we have about how the church is to function is found in 1 Corinthians 12–14.'[3]

---

[3] Bruce Bugbee, *What You Do Best in the Body of Christ* (Zondervan Publishing House, 1995), p. 92.

This approach, however, stretches the legitimacy of the text and aligns itself with the cessationists, who have institutionalised and rationalised these practices, consequently missing the valuable advice given by the apostle. Siegfried Schatzmann correctly assesses that it is not sufficient to juxtapose charisma and institution: the correct approach to a passage of Scripture is to determine what the writer intended, rather than superimposing preconceived ideas and theological bias to suit the reader's prejudices. Unfortunately, such balanced exegesis is rare, and the three passages under consideration here are generally commented on in a way that betrays the particular tradition to which the commentator belongs. Schatzmann comments: 'A definition of charisma must first of all reflect exegetical insights, not theological and dogmatic formulations of the institution.'[4]

The context of the passage is clearly believers meeting together, including for worship, and it is not meant to be a do-it-yourself kit list of gifts a believer somehow comes to possess. The believer, says Paul, is wholly dependent on the grace of God operating through the Holy Spirit, and it is he who 'gives them to each one, just as he determines' (1 Corinthians 12:11) when they 'come together' (11:18). The text that determines the context of this section of the letter starts at 11:17 and ends at 14:40, covering instructions about conduct and procedures when believers meet together. Initially Paul is discussing the attire of the participants, and there is no doubt that he is addressing problems which occurred when the Corinthian community 'came together' for worship (11:18, 33; 14:21, 26).

---

[4] Siegfried Schatzmann, *A Pauline Theology of Charismata* (Hendrickson Publishers, 1987), p. 8.

It seems that, when the Corinthians met together, the proceedings included Holy Communion, and this was being interrupted by women who were uninformed about the reason for being there. In addition, during these gatherings there was an incorrect and even abusive use of glossolalia. Paul's concern was that when they gathered, both men and women should reflect an attitude which expected, received and recognised the manifestations from the Holy Spirit, and not simply follow practices that had become divisive. The list at 12:8–10 describes the nature and form of these manifestations.

As part of his attempt to foster the right attitude, Paul offers corrective teaching on the use of glossolalia (1 Corinthians 14:5, 18–19, 23, 33, 36–38). Tongues, he maintains, are generally a private form of prayer and a means of enriching the life of the believer. When used in the context of corporate gatherings, however, he insists they are a means of edification and, as such, require interpretation. Hence, 'If anyone speaks in a tongue, two – or at the most three – should speak, one at a time, and someone must interpret' (14:27). All things should be done in a way that edifies the body, shows that they owe their origin to God, and acknowledges that it is his Holy Spirit who works all things through his people.

To underscore his corrective teaching, Paul says that every member of the church is eligible to be used by the Spirit when they gather: 'Now to *each one* the manifestation of the Spirit is given for the common good' (12:7, italics mine). This demonstrates the diversity of the occasion. The exercising of the charisma given to individual believers is not an end in itself. Rather, the most vital thing is for the body of the church, its members, to cultivate an attitude that recognises when the manifestations of the Holy Spirit take place, and to see them as a sign of his activity in their midst in order to build up their faith. The people gathered have no specific gifts to bring to such an occasion; it is the Holy Spirit who 'gives them to each one, just as he determines' (12:11).

Therefore, when believers come together in the name of Jesus, which can only be proclaimed if the Spirit is active in the life of a believer (12:3), their expectation should be that the Spirit will and can manifest his presence in the ways described (12:7–11). The emphasis is on the supernatural nature of the divine presence, as the Spirit wills, and not on any environment or ambience created by human and rational means. This is how gatherings of those who make up the church should be, says Paul to the Corinthians, and not like the sort of assemblies he has heard about from others. The same principles Paul speaks of here, with regard to believers gathering together, are still applicable today.

John Leach, a former curate at St Thomas's, offers a helpful matrix of the worship cycle in his book *Liturgy and Liberty*.[5] The matrix, shown below, was developed during his research on the expectation of the Holy Spirit interacting with believers. On the basis that Jesus is among those who are gathered in his name and desires to show to his people what he has done for them, there are corresponding side effects when Jesus becomes the centre of attention. As the cycle progresses, the worshippers' response also has side effects, which include pleasure for God and for the participants. Teaching and witness, as part of the cycle, ensure that the body is built up. God's response empowers, convicts, heals and converts, and the proclamation

---

[5] John Leach, *Liturgy and Liberty* (MARC, 1989), p. 38.

through worship that 'He is Lord' becomes an element of spiritual warfare. A person may not necessarily be in a receptive attitude, and may come to a gathering with a personal or even a selfish agenda. However, the presence of God becomes the powerful means of changing and enabling that person to see God at work as he manifests himself as described in 1 Corinthians 12. In this regard, the cycle commended by Leach (see page 88) becomes a useful way of helping Christians understand the process of the worship event.

One of the purposes of the Lifeskills course is to encourage members to come prepared when they gather in the name of Jesus, by putting into practice what Paul exhorts the Corinthians to do – namely, and as empowered by the Holy Spirit, 'When you come together [at a celebration, cluster or small group], everyone has a hymn, or a word of instruction, a revelation, a tongue or an interpretation' (1 Corinthians 14:26–33).

Those of the Reformed tradition contest such an interpretation with the argument that some of these gifts ceased at the end of the apostolic era and are therefore not relevant or even available to the church following the closure of the canon of Scripture. Their arguments, however, seem to strain the sense of the very texts they use to justify and maintain such a stance. Also, the church figures from history who are quoted as supporting this argument seem to be taken out of context. (Chapter 6 will discuss these issues in more detail.) Traditional denominational churches, while not holding such an extreme position, still often have difficulty in implementing the necessary changes which would allow an expectation that the Holy Spirit will operate among them in the way described by Paul. Their tendency is to be more preoccupied with maintaining correct liturgy and procedures during worship, and these

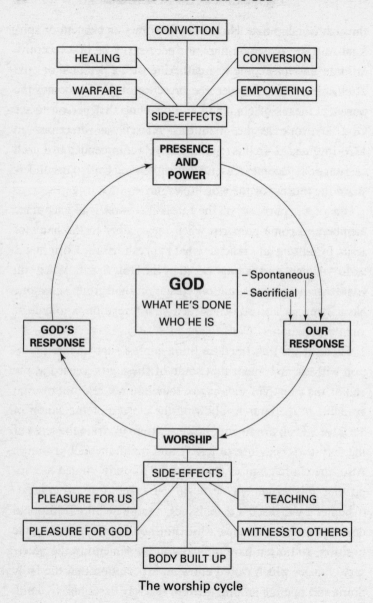

The worship cycle

concerns become obstacles to the freedom and alternative structure that Paul envisages.

Even at St Thomas's, it took us about 18 months after Mike Breen's arrival to come to terms with the principles of recognising that each member has a function within the church, as described in Romans and Corinthians. Most members understood the paradigm shift intellectually, but putting it into practice took longer. Worship and the exercise of the gifts of the Spirit had become normative through the influence of the charismatic renewal and VMI values, but the emphasis in the past had been to expect the worship leaders or clergy to be the initiators, or to give permission for gifts to be exercised. For worshippers to come prepared in advance to worship with the expectation that the Holy Spirit could use them required a much greater personal responsibility. This, in turn, created a different appreciation of the function of the clergy and worship leaders, because now there was an expectation that *all* were participants in the worship experience, rather than some taking the initiative and the rest being mere spectators. On occasions when a worshipper has a word or picture they feel has come from God and is relevant to those present, they are encouraged to share it with a moderator or leader before sharing it publicly.

Ephesians 4: the ministry gifts of the Holy Spirit

The Ephesians letter is believed by many scholars to be a circular letter to the churches of Asia and therefore not specific to local situations like the letters to Rome and Corinth. Commentators generally agree that the word 'Ephesus' is actually omitted in the original text, but is implied from references to the fact that the writer and the church had not yet met each other (Ephesians 1:15; 3:2–4). In the first three chapters Paul eulogises on the wonderful declaration of the purpose of God in Christ demonstrated in his church. Chapters 4–6 contain the practical outworking of those purposes through the people of God. The content of the letter, while containing many abstract concepts, is nonetheless a powerful and practical statement of how the church, under the headship of Jesus Christ, is the only way through which unity, reconciliation and peace can be brought into the world.

Chapter 4 is the passage pertinent to this book, in particular verses 7, 11 and 16. The context is the church as the body of Christ, created to operate as a result of their common experience of the Holy Spirit and faith in Jesus as the Lord of the church, all centred in the one God and Father of all. Most commentators agree that the grace of God imparted by Jesus to the believers is similar to that spoken of in Romans 12:3–6, with each believer being a recipient.

In Ephesians 4:7, Paul uses the same baseline to relate how God apportions his gift of grace to build up the body so that it might become mature and unified. Verse 11 describes how the apportioned gifts are identified, namely through members operating as apostles, prophets, evangelists, pastors and teachers to carry out the imperative of Ephesians 4:1–6. The grace given by Christ is a synonym for the Holy Spirit, with whom all the saints are 'sealed' (Ephesians 1:13–14; 4:30), and who empowers the whole church – 'each part does its work' (4:16) – to carry out their ministry to one another.

Opinions vary as to whether these designations, gifts or ministries are for the wider church or the local congregation. Some (such as Barth and Stott) deem them to be institutional offices in the church. Others say that apostles, prophets and evangelists are itinerant ministries and were part of the process in the founding of new churches, though not exclusively, whereas pastors and teachers are overseers of local congregations. Cessationist theologians argue that the ministries of the apostles and prophets ended when the canon of Scripture was formed. All seem to agree, however, that these are individual leadership positions in the church – and it is this interpretation which we at St Thomas's seek to dispute.

Paul is speaking of the practical outworking of the theology of the church, and textually it is legitimate and reasonable to assume that these ministries are extant today and also present in any church, regardless of size or denominational bias. The state church and its institutional form did not come into being until the fourth century, when the Emperor Constantine accepted Christianity as the preferred religion of the Roman Empire. Elements of this, known as the Christendom model, are still evident today and in the UK the Church of England with its links to civil government, the monarch as its governor and its role in the life of the nation is a prime example. The Lutheran church in Scandinavia and Germany occupies a similar position. When measured against what Paul describes in this letter, the modern church with its privilege and status is a poor representation of the model he portrays. That there were itinerant ministries present in the early church is not in question, and a logical conclusion of Paul's thesis here is that they were also present in the local church. Aside from the cessationist argument, which is difficult to sustain either biblically or intellectually (see Chapter 6), the Christendom interpretation is also flawed.

Ephesians 4:7 specifies who represents these gifts, namely 'each one of us', and verse 11 describes how they are distributed within the body. The Messiah, Jesus himself, is the gift after 'the unsearchable riches' of Ephesians 3:8; it is Christ expressed with all the power of his incarnation when he came as an apostle, prophet, evangelist, pastor and teacher, roles which he fulfilled most perfectly. Now, as the risen and ascended Lord, he gives of himself through his Spirit, without reservation, to the church. These gifts were not meant to be a substitute for his presence, but the mode by which he is present in the church. Without such empowerment, the church would be a hybrid, unable to reproduce, function as a body or be filled to the full, as promised to those who believed in him.

Contextually, there is no mention of institutional offices, gender, status or even leadership at this point in the letter. The church, whether in Corinth, Rome, Thessalonica, or elsewhere, has this grace apportioned to it to enable the members to operate with all the fullness of Christ's presence and power. If grace in this respect were only apportioned to those who were leaders, then the rest of the body would be impaired and crippled. Christ stated that he held nothing of himself back from those who confessed him as Lord; to do otherwise would be to deny himself, which is unthinkable.

Verse 12 goes on to record that these gifts are given 'to prepare God's people for works of service, so that the body of Christ may be built up'. Markus Barth, in his commentary *Ephesians 4–6*, suggests two concepts here.[6] One is designated by the insertion of a comma after 'works of service', which is reflected in the King James, New International and New American Standard Versions of the Bible. This punctuation

---

[6] Markus Barth, *Ephesians 4–6* (Doubleday, 1960), p. 479.

implies that apostles, prophets, evangelists, pastors and teachers, the ordained leadership of today, are given as gifts from
God to the church to prepare members to do the works of
service. Such an interpretation suggests at least a two-tiered
relationship: one tier above or outside the organism, the other
tier inferior and in need of sustenance, which can only be
gained from 'those above or outside'. The designation that
there is 'neither Jew nor Greek, slave nor free, male nor female,
for you are all one in Christ Jesus' (Galatians 3:28) seems to be
contradicted by such an interpretation.

The second concept, which reflects the interpretation of
Mike Breen, is that the Greek text does not permit such a distinction. Barth writes, 'When no comma is placed . . . then the
ministries of verse eleven are given to the church, in order that
"the saints" become "equipped" to carry out "the works of
service", even "the building".'[7]

Insight to support this argument can be extracted from
1 Corinthians 12:27–29, where apostles, prophets and teachers
are mentioned as being in the church. 'Now you are the body of
Christ, and each one of you is a part of it. And in the church God
has appointed first of all apostles . . .' Paul is saying here that in
the church at Corinth, the ministries he lists are part of the Holy
Spirit's equipping of the body. Paul's apostolic office had earlier
been questioned by the apostles at Corinth (1 Corinthians 9:1–6).
In chapter 12, the context being worship, the evidence is that all
Spirit-filled people are potentially prophets in that context (v. 10),
and in chapter 14 teachers appear as a gift given by the Holy Spirit
(v. 26). This accords with the view of Gordon Fee, who says:

---

[7] *Ibid.*

But in truth, Paul lists gifts and deeds and not persons. That probably suggests that the first three items, therefore, are not to be thought of as 'offices' held by certain 'persons' in the local church, but rather refer to 'ministries' as they find expression in various persons; likewise the following 'gifts' are not expressed in the church apart from persons, but are the gracious endowments given by the Spirit to various persons in the church for its mutual upbuilding.[8]

At St Thomas's, we believe that the five ministries of apostles, prophets, evangelists, pastors and teachers are to be found within the body of any church, regardless of its size or location. These descriptions reflect the base ministry (discussed in more detail in Chapter 5) of each individual member, as the Holy Spirit has apportioned grace.

In spite of his cessationist bias (which, incidentally, changed later on in his life), D.M. Lloyd-Jones commented on the word 'perfecting' in the King James Version or 'prepare' in the New International Version (Ephesians 4:12) by interpreting it as a medical term used in relation to the setting of dislocated bones. This is an image of the fractured relationship we have with the Father, caused by the fall. Part of the healing process – using the analogy of the body and its mechanism to 'grow and build itself up in love, as each part does its work' – is that apostles, prophets, evangelists, pastors and teachers are given to the church to show that the relationship with the Father has been reset, like that of a dislocated bone. Not only has the relationship been reset, but through the grace of Jesus the church is

---

[8] Gordon D. Fee, *God's Empowering Presence* (Hendrickson Publishers, 1994), pp. 189–190.

enabled to operate with all the fullness needed, 'so [that] the work is being done in every one of us, [and] we are being made to fit properly into our particular place in the Church, with the result that the whole body will function in a harmonious and satisfactory manner'.[9] To discover that these roles are not the preserve of the leadership but for all was initially daunting to some members of St Thomas's, but to their credit many went on to feel liberated and affirmed that their influence needed to be expressed and worked out in order to create a healthy church.

The Lifeskills course, as discussed in Chapter 7, has been designed to enable members to identify and understand what their ministry or gift is, and it introduces them to the dynamics of how people can minister in this way to the whole body. Using the three dimensions of UP, IN and OUT, the method should determine whether the anointing is evident (UP), attested and affirmed by the body (IN), and expressed to the body and the world (OUT).

[9] D.M. Lloyd-Jones, *Christian Unity* (Banner of Truth Trust, 1980), p. 199.

5

Characteristics of Church Members

In most walks of life, especially at work, people know their place and generally have a good idea of the responsibilities that go with the position they hold. This enables their company to operate effectively. Imagine the benefit it would be to the church in its mission if the same norms were applied to its members. If each member knew the part they were expected to play and were supported by a leadership which ensured they were resourced and equipped to fulfil the task of advancing the kingdom, then the result would be a growing and healthy church. Sadly, the opposite is often the case – and this is demonstrated by the fact that often 90 per cent of the tasks are done by 10 per cent of the members. This pattern persists, despite the analogy of the body being used extensively in the Scriptures to show that each person has his or her part to play. What a difference it would make if this were to be realised.

Often there are faithful souls in the church doing tasks for which they are unsuitable and ill-equipped, but they persevere because no one else is willing to take on those tasks. There are numerous references in the Bible which warn against shepherds or leaders of God's people not watching over their charges, yet in the workplace this is a normal operating procedure. During my service in the Royal Navy I was required to write regular assessments in the service documents of those who worked under me – including comments on their abilities and competence, how they fitted into the team, and issues which affected their general well-being. Also on record were all ships and shore establishments served during a sailor's career, details of next of kin, promotion qualifications and suitability for certain types of job – in effect the story of that individual's life. Sometimes a service record would show that a certain specialisation was counterproductive. I remember one humorous entry for a sailor who had been deemed unsuitable for submarine service and had to return to the surface fleet: 'This sailor plays the piano very well. Unfortunately this submarine does not have one.'

Having the right person in the right place is essential for a fighting service. The church is called to engage in the work and warfare of the kingdom, and the same criteria must therefore hold true. I am not suggesting an elaborate administrative structure in which everyone is under severe scrutiny, but rather, as discussed in the previous chapter, a practical outworking of the interpretation of the central passages relating to the gifts of the Holy Spirit for the members of the church. Romans 12 describes what members do in the church, whereas 1 Corinthians 12 describes the tools given by the Holy Spirit as he wills when members gather, whether in small or large groupings. These tools or gifts are made tangible when members understand which of the five types of person (listed in Ephesians 4:11) they have been created to be, by God's grace, so that they might operate effectively as a body. At St Thomas's many find it a liberating experience to discover the 'base' ministry that enables them to participate in 'prepar[ing] God's people for works of service, so that the body of Christ may be built up' (Ephesians 4:12).

Of course, this interpretation begs the question of how apostles, prophets, evangelists, pastors and teachers can be identified. Apostles and prophets are the most complex people to describe. Those in the early church were clearly figures of authority, and quite opposite in character to the excesses of some individuals offered as examples by the so-called New Church Movement. Evangelists are often described in stereotypical and caricatured images, even though they have been used effectively to win converts. Some have abused the office, however, bringing disrepute to the Lord of the church. Pastors and teachers are generally more acceptable terms, but in the main they are identified with leadership and authority figures. Let's have a look at each type of person in turn.

Apostles

The word 'apostle' is used for a messenger who can fulfil the role of an ambassador, a sent one, an envoy. It is also used in classical Greek of the commander of a naval force, and this description has even greater significance when applied to the New Testament role. Naval commanders have a considerable degree of authority at sea. Any mission they undertake has to allow for a wide-ranging degree of autonomy so that they can make decisions in every situation they encounter. They must be able to decide when to deviate from their set course during bad weather, they must be alert to all potential danger, and the risk of enemy attack requires them to be in a constant state of readiness. Provided they operate within the guidelines of the 'Fighting Instructions',[1] they are free to apply all the experience and authority with which they are endowed.

An associated word for apostle in Hebrew, *shaliach*, is used to describe a legal functionary empowered to transact business on behalf of others, for example a sale or a betrothal. A person's *shaliach* is therefore someone with the power of attorney, who can act as if they were that person themselves. The naval commander, by contrast, has a more general brief and the flexibility to meet any given situation, especially if it interferes with the mission of a particular voyage. The *shaliach*'s role is more task-orientated and does not permit any deviation or transfer of their responsibilities to another person. This latter description, being so limited, does not seem to justify its use to delineate the role of an apostle, and does not seem broad enough to apply to missionary activity.

There are three classes of apostle in the New Testament. First, there is Jesus, 'the apostle and high priest whom we confess' (Hebrews 3:1). Second, there are the twelve men chosen by Christ, 'that they might be with him and that he might send them out to preach and to have authority to drive out demons' (Mark 3:14). J.B. Lightfoot helpfully clarifies the question of whether subsequent apostles needed the same criteria as the first twelve:

---

[1] Most navies have, from ancient times, laid down a standard procedure on how and when they may engage an enemy, and these are often referred to as the 'Fighting Instructions'. Departure from these, especially if it entails defeat, results in the commander facing a summary trial and, if proved negligent, can lead to prison or even the death penalty.

Though it was necessary that an Apostle should have been an eye-witness to the Lord's resurrection, it does not follow that the actual *call to the Apostleship* should come from an outward personal communication with our Lord, in the manner in which the twelve were called. With Matthias it certainly was not so. The commission in his case was received through the medium of the church.[2]

The twelve apostles are regarded as the bridge between Jesus' ministry and the establishing of the church. However, for the most part, they perform the task given to them by Christ and then vanish from the scene. Not many of them wrote the inspired text of the New Testament. Their foundational role was preaching Christ, who was the founder of the church. Third, others designated as apostles appear in several passages, and they included women (Romans 16:7; Philippians 2:25; 2 Corinthians 8:23). There were also false apostles, who must have exercised enough authority and influence to require being singled out for correction (2 Corinthians 11:13; Revelation 2:2).

Have apostles ceased to exist? Markus Barth is emphatic that 'Ephesians 4 does not contain the faintest hint that the charismatic character of all church ministries was restricted to a certain period of church history and was later to die out'.[3] There is no evidence that they were appointed by divine ordinance to a position of authority within the church, and etymologically the word cannot be applied to a missionary. Paul designates the role of apostle as a charisma, a gift of the Holy Spirit.

---

[2] J.B. Lightfoot, *Saint Paul's Epistle to the Galatians* (Macmillan & Company, 1921), p. 98.

[3] Markus Barth, *Ephesians 4–6* (Doubleday & Co., 1960), p. 437.

At St Thomas's, the people who display the characteristics of apostles are generally those of a pioneering disposition. They travel light and seem to possess a clarity concerning their direction and destination. Often the details of how they will obtain their goal and carry out their ministry or task appear to be vague, especially to those for whom specifics are of prime importance before making any move of consequence. An example is of one member who had a very demanding job but also led one of the worship teams. He recognised the need for the team to look beyond just leading worship and reach out to those who were on the fringes of the church. He described them as 'strangers in our midst', not in a negative sense but as people who needed to be drawn more into the life and work of the church. After sharing it with the team some felt it was not for them, but those who decided to 'risk' such a move found within three months they had a cluster of 80-plus people. By the end of twelve months they grew to three clusters. Had they remained as only a worship team they would have missed out on a blessing.

Examples in the New Testament are the 72 disciples in Luke 10 who were given a mandate by Jesus to go ahead of him. They were warned they would be like lambs among wolves, and were told to take no purse, bag or sandals, but just to be alert to the 'people of peace' they would meet (Luke 10:3–7). Peter's encounter with Cornelius in Acts 10 has a similar ring. After receiving a vague and confused vision, he agreed to visit the home of a God-fearing Gentile, which many self-respecting Jews would consider anathema, and under the guidance of the Holy Spirit he was able to lead the whole household to faith. In Acts 13 Paul and Barnabas were commissioned by the church in Antioch to begin a work with the Gentiles. The text does not suggest that there was much tactical discussion as to how they were to be resourced on the way or how far they should travel. The strategy was clear: they were to go and proclaim the gospel. In these instances, the anointing for the task was evident (UP), it was attested by those who sent them (IN), and the mission to seek the lost was also clear (OUT).

It is interesting to note that there are not many of these figures mentioned in the Scriptures, which suggests that the percentage of apostles within any body is likely to be small. People who fulfil such roles have served the church throughout the centuries. In relation to their world and its circumstances there are always new horizons to be conquered. As visionaries, whether in high-profile positions or not, apostolic types have been uncomfortable bedfellows, especially to those of a settler mindset who prefer checks and balances to be in place before they invest time and energy in any given situation. The two can complement each other, however: pioneers like the Pilgrim Fathers mapped out whole new frontiers, which were later turned into towns and cities by those of a settler disposition. John Wesley and William Carey had similar visionary qualities, and such people are also present – albeit in 'micro' form – in every local church. Personality and drive are not a measure of their status, however. The apostles are placed within the body as part of the economy of God to enable the church to move out from its comfort zone and fulfil the Great Commission.

Prophets

Prophets have been a feared grouping within the church since earliest times. Montanism, which broke upon the church in the second century, so disrupted its life and witness that since then there has been a reticence to embrace the practice of prophecy, which in many respects has become consigned to the edges of church life. Eusebius records some of the effects of Montanus's behaviour. When he prophesied, he 'began to babble and utter strange sounds, that is to say, prophesying contrary to the manner which the Church had received from generation to generation from the beginning'.[4]

A fear of such behaviour is present even today, and in conservative evangelical circles the concern seems to stem from the danger of prophecy being given a higher prominence than Scripture. It is clear, however, that prophecy cannot be above the authority of the Bible, because we are told in the New Testament that all prophecy must be tested and weighed against Scripture, and by the experience of the prophets themselves (1 Corinthians 14:29). Like other gifts used when the church gathers, it is an indication of the Holy Spirit manifesting his power. Thomas Aquinas is helpful in recognising some of the limitations which apply when this gift is used:

> The human mind will never be anything but a 'defective instrument' in the hands of God, and even in the optimum case in which it has full awareness of having supernatural visions and a divine light for interpreting them, its knowledge will always fall short of the intentions of the Holy Spirit.[5]

That God is in the business of communicating with his people when they pray, read the Bible and meet together is not in

---

4 J. Stevenson, *A New Eusebius* (SPCK, 1963), p. 108.
5 Paul Synave and Pierre Benoit, *Prophecy and Inspiration. A Commentary on the Summa Theologica 11–11, Questions 171–178* (Desclee Company, 1961), p. 76.

question. By definition, prophecy must also be seen as a legitimate means by which he communicates. It comes in the form of an office, a person, as indicated in Romans 12, and is listed among the gifts present when believers gather together, as well as being named as a ministry. It employs the intellect as well as the empowering of the Holy Spirit. Prophecies do not always involve entirely new or fresh insight. Often prophecy is related to images and ideas conceived in the distant or recent past, which, under the influence of the Spirit, are rearranged to reveal hitherto unknown truths as a message for a given situation. In this regard prophecy differs from the preparation a preacher makes for a sermon, which has a specific aim in mind. Spontaneous revelation given by the Lord has not been researched in the same way that a sermon has been prepared. It is not that one is superior or inferior to the other, but rather that in each case the function and manifestation of the Holy Spirit are necessarily different.

The danger of the gift of prophecy is that the church and the individuals operating in this role can easily become too focused on the experience, emotion and blessing it brings, thus nullifying its effectiveness to the body. Instead of being led by the Holy Spirit to serve the kingdom and benefit from the power that comes from obedience, the prophets risk becoming objects of ridicule. Those who operate regularly in this mode may find themselves being sought out by people who are looking to them to function more like fortune-tellers than channels of God's word. People in this category, as Paul says, 'treat prophecies with contempt' (1 Thessalonians 5:20).

Part of the building up of the church, as enjoined in Ephesians 4, is that the body of the church, as well as individuals within it, should act in a prophetic manner. Often, however, this is inverted so that only ordained clergy and leaders perform the task – and because such an approach goes against the way this ministry was intended to be exercised, it is ineffective. At St Thomas's, the risk of allowing members of the body to expect and receive this empowering of the Spirit, as well as recognising individuals anointed to serve as prophets in the church – with all the attendant implications of inexperience and unaccustomed practice – has moved our sense of the importance of mission to a new level. Those who act as 'watchmen' in this way help the church to be more alert to the need to be prophetic to our community and city.

Evangelists

'Evangelism is one of those emotionally charged words which sends shivers of guilt running up and down the average church member's spine,' says Steve Sjogren.[6] It conjures up images of vast stadiums full of potential converts who will 'walk the aisle' in response to an articulate and gifted evangelist inviting people to make a decision for Jesus, often to the accompaniment of a choir singing a hymn such as 'Just as I am'. Other images are of the faithful doing door-to-door visitations, or the embarrassment of being part of an amateur piece of street theatre in a shopping precinct.

All these approaches have validity, but they require time, effort and resources that most local churches do not have. Sometimes the suggestion of joining with other denominations in order to generate enough impetus to hold a quality event poses the dilemma that such collaboration might dilute the

---

[6] Steve Sjogren, *Conspiracy of Kindness* (Vine Books, 1993), p. 34.

content and style of the message by compromising on some fine
doctrinal issue. Such a posture feeds hidden prejudice, while at
the same time compounding the guilt of 'not being evangelistic
enough'.

There is no escaping the need for the church to undertake
evangelism, and it is hard to ignore the seriousness of the
command to go and make disciples. The question is, how can it
be done effectively and meaningfully, without producing the
deep sense of failure that most attempts seem to bring?

In Ephesians 4:11, evangelism is narrowed down to a ministry which comes as a grace given by the Holy Spirit to individuals. The evidence of the New Testament indicates that the
evangelists did not depend solely on staging events, as is often
the modern practice. Some commentators suggest that these
individuals had full-time positions as leaders within the church,
the equivalent of today's ordained ministers. In some cases this
was certainly true, but it was frequently the ordinary members
of a local church who, through their witness and lifestyle, demonstrated the life-changing effect of the gospel.

Such witness did not rely on crusades, evangelism drives or
any kind of event-orientated methodology. So effective was
these people's evangelism that Luke records, 'All the believers
used to meet together in Solomon's Colonnade. No-one else
dared join them, even though they were highly regarded by the
people. Nevertheless, more and more men and women believed
in the Lord and were added to their number' (Acts 5:12–14).
The message was consistent. Their faithful witness under hard-
ship showed that they would not be cowed into denying their
Lord. Their methodology for evangelism under these circumstances was subservient to their local cultural setting, even
when it meant persecution (Acts 10:23–48; 19:25–34; 26:1–31;

Philippians 1:12–14). Failure does not seem to have been an issue in terms of the evangelistic expansion of the early church. Conversely, in the Western church today, fear of failure takes the specific form of the fear of looking foolish. The 'event' aspect of mass evangelism was rare in the early church, so why is it the style which most readily comes to the fore today?

In terms of evangelists as depicted in Ephesians 4:11, people anointed with this grace seem to be those who are undeterred when it comes to sharing their faith with unbelievers. This is a level above the witnessing to which all members of the church are called. It draws on the natural ability of those who are disposed towards speaking about Christ, in that the Holy Spirit compels their listeners to want to know the one who has given these evangelists such boldness and certainty about the Saviour of whom they speak. We have a member who whenever she travels by bus into town readily engages in conversation with the person sitting next to her. By the time the bus has reached the next stop the conversation has flowed easily and comfortably into her sharing she is a member of St Thomas's. By the next stop there is usually an invitation to attend one of the services, and as she always carries some literature with our logo, times of services, etc., she has passed it on. There is seemingly no effort in her ability to share in this way, because she is an outward, effervescent type who loves talking to people and sharing herself with them without causing offence.

In many respects evangelists are pioneering types, not afraid to move into new environments – and in fact this is what gives them the greatest pleasure and sense of fulfilment. On another level, however, they have a settler mindset because they recognise the context of the situations they seek to evangelise and know that their converts need to be grounded in the faith, becoming part of a fellowship that will give a new stability to their lives. With the grace they possess, they are usually unable to take an enquirer or convert beyond the first stage of commitment, and it is then the role of pastors and teachers to take those converts on to become effective disciples.

Using the questionnaire given in Appendix A at seminars led by St Thomas's in over 40 churches in the UK, I have discovered that between 12 and 15 per cent of members are gifted in this way. This discovery is not dissimilar to the research results of Christian A. Schwarz, set out in his book *Natural Church Development*. Paul's emphasis is that when people are able to define their role and be used in the way God has designed, it will have the same effect as in the early church, when 'the Lord added to their number daily those who were being saved' (Acts 2:47).

The next two types of people, pastors and teachers, seem to be more accessible roles, and are generally identified with leaders. In the text of Ephesians 4 the definite article is missing at this point and whether they are separate or joint examples of grace could be considered an open question. To maintain consistency, we prefer to consider them as separate people types and, like all the other roles, to include rank-and-file members as well as leaders. They form the largest part of the body because of the input needed for those who come to faith through evangelism and require the care and teaching commensurate with their newly professed faith.

Pastors

This caring dimension of the church involves knowing those who need that care and input to enable them to grow in 'their most holy faith'. Pastors are an essential part of the process of discipleship, and are there in the body to provide love and care to those buffeted by the stresses of life and the attack of the enemy.

For such a task to be in the hands of leaders only would be an intolerable burden for them to bear. Elsewhere leaders are called elders (*presbyteroi* – Acts 20:17; 1 Peter 5:1) or bishops (*episkopi* – Acts 20:28), and the use of the word 'pastor' to describe a leader was not the vogue when Paul wrote Ephesians. The term was used of a leader, ruler or military commander in classical Greek, and in the Old Testament it was used to describe a shepherd, a role usually carried out by members of the family or hired hands. The expectation was that such people would be responsible, capable of exercising caution, patience, care and honesty in all their dealings. Within the church family, such people would be given grace to exercise a spirit of humility, reflecting an ability to be part of the guarding of hearts and minds as enabled by the Holy Spirit. Such Christ-centred people by definition have the ability to be an encouragement to those who are weak in the faith. An example of those with such a disposition is the people who form part of our counselling team.

Teachers

Like pastors, teachers are those able to lead at all levels, but the role is not necessarily exclusive in this respect. Teachers are those who have the ability to draw on the wisdom of their own walk with Christ, as well as on the heritage and history of the past. They act to correct false doctrine and help to feed the consciences of the church members, in order that they might live righteous lives before God and their community. In the discipleship process they have a major task in forming attitudes, promoting habits and building the body up to maturity.

Like pastors, teachers are those who create the structures and fabric of the society of the church, and they are clearly at the settler end of the spectrum. Unlike those at the pioneering end, they do not relish change unless there are strong and responsible reasons for it. Nevertheless, both pastor and teacher types are usually the best suited to act as mentors. In our postmodern society in particular, they are essential for the way they can tap into a past which has insights into a stability of life apparently now lost to the Generation Xers. That is why it is important to help members of the Builder generation make the adjustments necessary to cross the communication divide, because there is a willing audience waiting for them.

What lies at the heart of Paul's instructions in Ephesians 4 – as well as in Romans 12 and 1 Corinthians 12 – is not that the church should be a forum in which democratic equality is maintained, nor that those recognised and anointed as leaders should be somehow excluded. The way leadership should be conducted is the subject of other passages in the New Testament, but it is not Paul's concern in this section of Ephesians. The concern is with order in the church, rather than with church order. All members, Paul indicates, have grace apportioned by Christ, and his desire is that they should reflect its effects in the ways in which they think about themselves and others.

6

A Paradigm Shift in the Theology of Ministry

St Thomas's seeks to affirm that the church of today remains a thoroughly charismatic institution. It is therefore necessary to address some of the issues related to cessationism, which argues that miracles or extraordinary charismata were terminated at or near the end of the apostolic age. Set against this is the belief that such charismata are and should be normative in contemporary church life and ministry. This conviction is becoming increasingly widespread, especially in our postmodern society. According to a survey conducted by Gallup, 79 per cent of Americans believe in miracles – apparently overcoming their propensity to rely solely on rational knowledge in this regard. In addition, 41 per cent said they had experienced something that might be described as miraculous. The number of people who both believe in and have experience of miracles is highest among those who say that religion is 'very important' in their lives.[1]

---

[1] George Gallup, Jr and D. Michael Lindsay, *Surveying the Religious Landscape* (Morehouse Publishing, 1999), pp. 25–27.

Permanent or temporary?

An early form of cessationism was directed at Jesus. Jon Ruthven, in his research on this subject, indicates that from the Maccabean era onwards there was an ambivalence towards prophecy and miracles, which developed into a belief that the Spirit's activity had ended.[2] This was particularly prevalent at the time of Jesus among the rabbinical school, which had developed Judaism into a monotheistic religion based on a written Torah using scholastic interpretation. Part of the accusation at Jesus' trial was that he had contravened the law, as detailed in Deuteronomy 13 and 18, forbidding the performance of a sign or wonder which might lead people astray to false gods – on the basis that God no longer intervened in the affairs of Israel through prophecy and signs and wonders. The activity demonstrated by Jesus was therefore demonic and even pagan.

Historical developments

In the second century, Montanism, with its emphasis on prophecy, scolded the church for being 'unspiritual', because the church rejected the Montanists' claim that they were the mouthpieces of the Holy Spirit. In effect, the worst excess of this movement was their prophesying, which they deemed to be the equivalent of creating a new Bible.

As the church became more of an institution, it developed a tendency to transmute the supernatural and charismatic activities of the early church into what was deemed to be the 'normal' ministry of the church. Prophecy became defined as

---

[2] Jon Ruthven, *On the Cessation of the Charismata* (Sheffield Academic Press, 1993), pp. 25–26.

preaching or teaching, and miracles became metaphors for regeneration, in which the spiritually blind saw the light of the gospel intellectually, and the lame walked the paths of righteousness. Speaking in tongues was replaced by oratory and music, while revealed knowledge was incorporated into the catechetical teaching of new converts and the theological training given to the clergy, who were to lead the laity of the church. In time this became a helpful way of explaining why charismatic activity, as described in the New Testament, was no longer normative.

In the thirteenth century, Aquinas asserted that Jesus and the disciples had worked miracles to prove the sufficiency of the faith once for all and, after they had done so, miracles were no longer required. He did suggest, however, that believers of great sanctity could, at times, demonstrate further proof of the miraculous gifts of the Spirit. This led to an unhealthy veneration of such figures when they were alive, and after death their tombs and relics became places of pilgrimage which were exploited by the Roman Church. A prime example of such exploitation was the sale of indulgences to finance the building of St Peter's in Rome, one scheme among many aimed at raising money to service the needs of the church. These abuses eventually served as a springboard into the events which led to the Protestant Reformation.

The reformer John Calvin understood that miracles were done to accredit the Bible and those who proclaimed its message and derived the doctrines central to the Christian faith. This was in reaction to claims from the Roman Church, which was using the notion of contemporary miracles to bolster its plea for apostolic succession, as well as being a response to the Spirit-inspired 'excesses' of other radical reformers. In relation to Ephesians 4, Calvin's contention was that apostles, prophets and evangelists were not for today. Nonetheless, he qualified this by saying, 'The Lord raised these up at the beginning of his Kingdom, *and now and again revives them as the need demands.*'[3]

The triumph of reason

These interpretations of the restricted role of the Holy Spirit in terms of intervention into the world's affairs gathered momentum in the eighteenth century under the influence of the era known as the Enlightenment. During this period religious authority, and in particular biblical authority, was replaced by human authority, largely on the basis of perception and reason. The developers of natural science argued that God had ordered nature to operate by fixed laws, and this led to the perception of a closed cosmology in which there was no possibility of God's intervention. Scholars maintained that all happenings had an empirical basis which could be explained by common sense and rational thinking. Following this philosophy, Deists challenged the possibility that miracles, whether in Bible times or subsequently, had ever happened at all.

Undoubtedly, people's minds are shaped by the world in which they live. Their worldview reflects the culture around them, acting as a lens which helps them to clarify and formulate actions and give definition to reality. Today, those over 35 years old who have been educated in the West have, without realising it, become so secularised that they automatically focus

---

[3] John Calvin, *Institutes of the Christian Religion*, ed. John T. McNeill, trans. Ford Lewis Battles (The Westminster Press, 1960), p. 1056, italics mine.

on the temporal and the things which bring immediate pleasure or success. This has resulted in a loss of the supernatural and transcendent dimension of the human experience. Materialism features high on the agenda, so that the pursuit of comfort and the money to buy it has become a priority of life. This has fuelled the concept that modern humankind is in charge of its destiny – each individual looking out for number one. Questions of ultimate purpose feature less often, and the measure of real goodness and happiness is often expressed in terms of material possessions. Consequently, only those things which are material and 'real' are defined as constant, dependable and acceptable.

The result is that science and technology have become more important, by giving the appearance of being successful and at the same time seeming to transcend religious, cultural and international barriers more effectively than organised religion. Physical phenomena, along with social and psychological disciplines, have become the means of providing a more developed understanding of the world. Extending the Enlightenment approach, experience has to be subject to scientific experiment to verify whether it is trustworthy and repeatable. This has contributed to a worldview in which there is nothing that cannot be understood, and all things can be explained: the simpler the hypothesis, the greater the likelihood of it being true.

The belief in the potential of expressing such a philosophy through individual and corporate power appears to have led humankind to feel that it is we who have made the world a more secure place in which to live. Religion, and in particular Christianity, has been relegated to the extremities of life – where modernity has not been able to provide adequate answers to such issues as death, or the problem of guilt and its associated

maladies. Its hold on even these extremities is becoming more
tenuous, however. Advances in medical science have contributed
to longevity. In the field of psychology, where there is now a
greater measure of understanding of some root causes of guilt,
neurosis, depression and other psychiatric ills, partial control of
these conditions has been fairly successful through the use of
therapy and drugs. Some argue that further research and development in these and associated fields will marginalise religion
and the supernatural dimension even further.

Right and wrong, under such circumstances, are defined by
a culture in which there are now no moral absolutes and relativism has become the governing factor. Reason is the chief
guide to most matters of life, and decisions are therefore not
dependent on spiritual values, the eternal dimension or the
things of God. God thus appears to be an illusion, and we are
encouraged to believe that we have enough information and
resources to manage our own affairs effectively without intervention from any deity. The primary value is all on observation
and intellectual knowledge, as opposed to experiential and
metaphysical knowledge. Religion has therefore come to play a
minor role, as an acceptable outlet for humanity's spiritual
needs, but not essential.

The effect on the church

This secular worldview has affected the church, not so much in
a confrontational way, but more by the pervasive glorification
of nature and reason, and by an intrusion of the sceptical
mindset into the realms beyond science and modernity where
access to truth comes through faith. Given the overwhelming
achievements of modern science and technology, the prophets

of secularism seem able to call down considerable fire on their offerings. By contrast, the church has retreated in the face of such apparent superiority, and in many ways has lost its nerve. This in turn has bolstered the belief that humankind has the ability to provide for itself, and there is therefore less of a requirement to seek security in God. To expect or even suggest the likelihood of divine intervention tends to produce a negative reaction, and this is aggravated by a general loss of awareness that we need to live in this age by the values of the age to come.

When understood from the perspective of modernity, human beings are split off from the spiritual, emotional, intuitive and imaginative properties by which God can be known. Rationalism and materialism have dethroned God as the Creator and have removed the significant place Christ holds as the special revelation of the Father's love and plan for the well-being of humankind. This devalues faith as the access road to truth, and relativism undermines God's order for human life. While this may not completely erase God from the Christian's mind, of course, continual exposure to such a worldview has had the effect of making God a remote, ultimate cause rather than the personal God who is close at hand. The process of living comes under the domain of the natural, with no expectation of the intervention of the hand of God. Consequently, many in the modern church, while still retaining a belief in the existence of God, have tended mentally to disconnect him from his kingship of creation.

When Jesus inaugurated the kingdom, he demonstrated experientially the validity of the kingdom message. He challenged the kind of unbelief described above by demonstrating the loving presence and activity of a God in whom his hearers believed, but whom they could not see. Many Christians seem able to make a partial exception for God in the area of experience, and even at times to take him seriously in this regard. Often, however, the mindset which would allow belief in such things as healings, power encounters, angels, demons and Satan is simply not there, and these matters are relegated to the 'fairy tale' category.

Biblical criticism

The naturalistic perspective is reinforced in the church by some scholars who suggest that such supernatural language and activity of God are not for today. The tradition of 'biblical criticism' in liberal theology during the nineteenth century added fuel to this argument. Applying general historical principles to biblical documents, this school of thought regarded the Bible's contents as events recorded by human means without necessarily being divinely inspired. Questions were asked regarding the relationship of contemporary oral and written sources, their trustworthiness, and how the authors used them. In New Testament studies this became a tool for those who, in their quest for the historical Jesus, wished to substantiate their claim that Christ died in despair and disillusionment as a deluded first-century apocalyptic.

Positive advantages were also gained from this methodology. It provided valuable insights into the historical, cultural, linguistic, philosophical and theological background of the Scriptures, and confirmed the essential accuracy of the material on which the older translations were based, including the King James Version of 1611. It did, however, undermine the confidence of large sections of the church concerning the Bible's role in the process of special revelation, and unwittingly contributed to contention about the validity of the purpose and work of the Holy Spirit.

The rediscovery of the Spirit

The emergence of Pentecostalism in 1906, and in particular the Azusa Street revival in Los Angeles, forged the link between Spirit baptism and the gifts of the Holy Spirit – thereby stirring up a cauldron of strife. This rediscovery of the experiential and supernatural dimension of the faith caused many problems for a church already affected by rationalism and secularism and thus lacking a category for such manifestations. It led to accusations of emotionalism, 'enthusiasm' and even demon possession from those opposed to such displays in public worship.

In response to the ascendancy of the liberal school, B.B. Warfield, H.C.G. Moule of Durham and the Scotsman James Orr published *The Fundamentals* in 1909. This publication upheld the verbal inspiration and infallibility of Scripture, the virgin birth, the atoning work of the cross, the resurrection 'with the same body', and the miracles of Jesus. In 1918, however, Warfield's publication *Counterfeit Miracles* emphasised a denial of post-biblical miracles and stated that the exercise of the gifts of the Holy Spirit, the power to expel demons and the ability to speak in tongues were credentials exclusively belonging to those authoritative agents of God who were active when the church was founded. This was a capitulation to the rising secularism which had now invaded the church as well as society, adding to general doubts about the supernatural dimension of the faith.

Subsequent factions retreated into a defensive, obscurantist, anti-scholarly and anti-intellectual mode known as 'fundamentalism'. While this was not the original intention of the scholars involved, Warfield's response to the gifts of the Holy

Spirit as experienced by the Pentecostals demonstrated his inability to break the mould of Enlightenment thinking under which he had been educated.

As a consequence, Pentecostals were marginalised by mainstream Christianity, and Pentecostalism became the gospel for the poor, the Afro-Americans and those on the edges of society. Such isolation was arguably what led them to speak of a two-stage process of conversion, whereby repentance and faith in Christ required a second baptism of the Holy Spirit, evidenced by tongues. It is not unreasonable that such an interpretation should be applied as the norm for the outworking of the faith, as this experience was not reflected in the wider church and needed a category by which it could be defined. In turn, for some branches of Pentecostalism, it became a tenet necessary for Christian witness and discipleship.[4]

The Christendom interpretation of Ephesians 4

With this background, it is scarcely surprising that many theologians and scholars are sceptical of the implications of Romans 12, 1 Corinthians 12–14 and Ephesians 4 as discussed in Chapter 4. The roots of such thinking are actually found in Platonic philosophy, which set forth a series of arguments for the existence of a 'divine' reason in the world. Fundamental to

---

[4] One Pentecostal theologian expresses this viewpoint as follows: 'Glossolalia is of greater importance than the other Gifts of Grace, and is, at the same time, evidence of the Spirit baptism, a means of gaining Christian assurance, and was also in the beginning thought to be necessary for mission work' (Nihls Bloch-Hoell, *The Pentecostal Movement* [Allen & Unwin, 1964], p. 142).

this philosophy is the distinction between *being* and *becoming*. In the material world inhabited by humankind, everything is subject to change and decay – it is always *becoming* something else. In contrast there is the realm of *being*, which is eternal and unchanging. For Plato, this meant that reality is the realm of the unchanging, while the transient and material world is merely a pale reflection of that reality. The material world, being temporal and mutable, is therefore inferior, and even to be despised, because it can only be seen as a shadow of the eternal, unchanging realm of reality where God is.

An extension of this argument is that God cannot deal directly with a changing world, and human beings need a mediator if they are to comprehend God. The figure known as the Logos was therefore said to assume this role. The Logos, as reason and word, was believed to be separate from God and inferior to him. It was by the Logos that human beings could know the truth about God, because they are body and soul: the body belongs to this world of becoming and change, while the soul is a 'divine spark' from the world of being and is rational. Just as the divine Word or Logos indwells and controls the universe, so the body is indwelt and controlled by the Logos and, as a consequence, the existence of God can be discovered.

What kind of God?

It is difficult to comprehend what kind of God lies at the heart of such a philosophy. If it is possible that he can be discovered by reason, then he must, by definition, be inferior to a wholly transcendent God who must reveal himself if he is to be known. The Christian belief, by contrast, is that God the Father sent his Son Jesus to demonstrate that he chose to reveal himself, to reach out to us, as manifested in the Scriptures and through his Holy Spirit.

That Plato diligently sought after truth is not in question; the weakness lies in his inability to offer a clear perception of a personal God. There is nothing in his writings which equates with the kind of communication indicated by the phrase 'thus saith the Lord', because, from a Platonic perspective, God is discovered by humankind, whereas, in the Bible, it is God who finds them. The consistent theme of the biblical testimony is of God seeking to disclose and reveal himself to his people, and it is this which distinguishes Christian belief in the revelation of Jesus as the Son of God from Platonism. The dilemma for those believers who seek to develop their corporate personal relationship with God using such a framework is that, at best, knowledge of God is propositional rather than personal. Jesus prayed for all people, 'that they may know you, the only true God, and Jesus Christ, whom you have sent' (John 17:3). It was Jesus' intention that people should know God in a filial relationship, one in which they would be discerning agents of his will.

A question of integrity

The argument concerning reason was developed by Thomas Aquinas in the thirteenth century, and forms the basis of Roman Catholic theology today. Aquinas argued that it was possible for philosophers to establish a number of important truths about God, such as his nature and existence, but an understanding of the Trinity, atonement, grace, worship, prayer, and so on, could only be appropriated by faith. The latter comes by revelation and by the authority of the church, as the custodian of supernatural truths. In this way a two-step process of Christianity came about, first through philosophy and then through faith. One part was built on reason, the other part on the ministry of the sacraments of the church, resulting in a general optimism concerning the values of human reason.

According to Thomistic theology, human nature was wounded at the fall by the loss of their supernatural gifts, but the physical ability of human reasoning was not destroyed. Reason can thus reach out to God. G.C. Berkouwer cites De Vovel, who states, 'Mankind can get a preliminary but true knowledge of God by anthropological analysis by virtue of their non-depraved reasoning.'[5] This requires a high doctrine of humankind as moral beings, however, because it assumes that they will act with integrity when reasoning about God. History abounds with examples of the waywardness of human beings whose emotions are often 'irrational', especially when dictated by reason. Moral responsibility under these conditions becomes diluted and sin can easily be reduced to a point where it becomes merely a mistaken search for God. Aquinas's logic under-estimates human weakness, because it assumes integrity in the use of rational faculties.

Apportioning grace

If such a gloss is transposed onto the interpretation of apostles, prophets, evangelists, pastors and teachers as listed in Ephesians 4, it can easily be deduced that they are the officers, the ordained clergy, who have been anointed and trained to build up the body, and to whom the privilege and burden of building up the saints is exclusively assigned. The laity passively receive the means of salvation and grace through the sacraments, they are cared for,

---

[5] G.C. Berkouwer, *General Revelation* (Eerdmans, 1955), p. 74.

they are given ethical instruction through preaching and sound doctrine, and discipline is administered to them. With respect, St Thomas's would suggest that this attitude has contributed to the distortion of the texts concerning the gifts and ministries given by the Holy Spirit. The distinction between clergy and laity is a Christendom interpretation, and the real sense of these texts is that all are 'clergy' appointed by God for a ministry to the church and to the world in which they live. Otherwise, the 'laity' are reduced to the role of consumers.

If God apportions his grace in the way described in Ephesians 4, and believers can reach out to him and commune with him as described in Romans 12 and 1 Corinthians 12, then grace, when engaged and appropriated as God intended, is bound to go beyond the limited spirituality and understanding which originates in a small part of the human brain. The fourteenth-century author of *The Cloud of Unknowing* comments:

> Whenever the feeling of grace is withdrawn, pride is always the cause; not necessarily actual pride, but potential pride that would have arisen if the feeling had not been withdrawn. Sometimes it is withheld because of carelessness. Sometimes our Lord delays the feeling of grace quite deliberately because he wants, by such delays, to make it grow and to be more appreciated.[6]

This *other* dimension of God must therefore be outside the capability of human resources and requires, somehow, a transference of God's personality to human life if we are to be able to appropriate this grace. The Holy Spirit becomes the one

---

[6] Betty Radice (ed.), *The Cloud of Unknowing and Other Works* (Penguin, 1961), p. 151.

through whom that transference is accomplished. Paul says, 'No-one can say, "Jesus is Lord," except by the Holy Spirit' (1 Corinthians 12:3). This leads logically to the conclusion that humankind has been made for more than earthly life can offer, even the life of the ordained ministry. When we embrace the grace of God which is available to us as believers, 'the Spirit himself testifies with our spirit that we are God's children' (Romans 8:16).

Gifts from the fullness of grace

Many churches and their leaders, even if they do not articulate their opposition to the work of the Holy Spirit in the kind of philosophical terms outlined above, are nevertheless influenced by the biblical commentaries and theological works that put forward such viewpoints. Their real dilemma is not so much to do with the decision of whether or not to reject the cessationist argument and to believe in the operation of the Holy Spirit, but more to do with how they should understand the manifestations which accompany the Spirit's presence. This is an understandable problem, because such things are not the normative experience for their pattern of church life and practice.

The idea that the Holy Spirit can be invoked is generally contested on the grounds that the Spirit is sovereign and cannot be manipulated. Critics argue that participants are subjected to auto-suggestion, hypnosis and even mass hysteria, and such was the media coverage of the meetings held at the Toronto Airport Christian Fellowship, a former Vineyard Church, in January 1994. At an ordinary meeting of the church fellowship, an outpouring of the Holy Spirit resulted in scenes reminiscent of the Wesley meetings during the Great Awakening of the eighteenth century, and the manifestations included laughter, crying, shaking, prophecy and, in some cases, animal noises. The latter was often a feature of revival meetings in the Midwest of America. In many respects, there was nothing unusual in such manifestations, given the tradition of Vineyard Church practice. Nonetheless, on this occasion the church leadership, under John Arnott, decided to meet each subsequent evening to wait upon God and try to discern what they felt he was saying to the church about its ministry. Over the ensuing months, the news of these gatherings attracted visitors from all over the world, hungry for a fresh experience of God. The church still attracts several hundred people each day. Other centres in Pensacola, Florida, Lagos, Nigeria and many cities in South America are experiencing similar manifestations with large attendances. The expectation is that when the Holy Spirit is asked to come, he comes, and signs follow the effects of his presence.

Learning to expect

Church traditions which have never experienced or even expected such manifestations are understandably reticent about moving in this direction. It is, however, true to say that similar language and expectations do form part of their regular liturgy. One example is the Anglican Church's Rite A Holy Communion, as set out in *The Alternative Service Book*. Using the Eucharistic Prayer, the priest declares, 'The Lord is here,' to which the worshippers answer, 'His Spirit is with us.' The Third Eucharistic Prayer includes the words, 'Send the Holy Spirit on your people and gather into one in your kingdom . . .' The expectation that the Spirit is present and invoked through liturgy may be a matter of intellect and fine doctrine, but in the strictest sense of the words, the Spirit's presence is here assumed and invoked by celebrant and worshipper alike. It is another question entirely whether space and time are built into the service to accommodate the expectation that the Holy Spirit will manifest his presence as requested and interact with the worshipping community.

The church at large and those who lead it need to resolve the question of whether Jesus, as the mediator of the new covenant, is still enabling the church to do what he promised it should do when he said, 'I tell you the truth, anyone who has faith in me will do what I have been doing. He will do even greater things than these, because I am going to the Father' (John 14:12). The crucial part of this paradigm shift comes in exercising the will to practise and take literally Jesus' assertion, 'If anyone chooses to do God's will, he will find out whether my teaching comes from God or whether I speak on my own' (John 7:17). This is in marked contrast to the anthropocentric viewpoint held by much of the church and society today, in which humankind – our moral and religious experience, our social and cultural awareness – is the all-absorbing centre of attention.

The cycle of grace

The church must move on from its preoccupation with itself and its confused experience of God, and come to terms with the effect and significance of the grace he offers. I found the diagram shown below a helpful tool in processing this idea. The 'cycle of grace' starts with the *acceptance* of what Christ has done for all believers by his grace and obedience to the commands he left to his church. Such a proposition is enshrined in the orthodox creeds of the church and is a declaration of faith that Christians have been created to be discerning agents of God's grace. John Hick offers this explanation:

Thus the primary religious perception, or basic act of religious interpretation, is not to be described as either a reasoned conclusion or an unreasoned hunch that there is a God. It is, putatively, an apprehension of the divine presence within the believer's human experience. It is not an inference to a general truth, but a 'divine human encounter', a mediated meeting with the living God.[7]

The second stage of the cycle is the *sustenance* of the first step. Jesus demonstrated this supremely by his prayer life and worship of his heavenly Father. Nights of prayer and continual

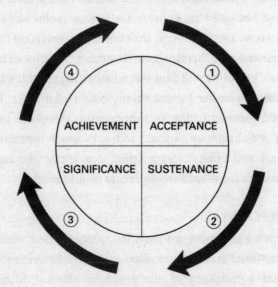

The cycle of grace

sacrifice and discipline showed that his need and desire was for God his Father, that he might do his will.

Practising the presence of God produced the third element in

---

[7] John Hick, *Faith and Knowledge* (Fontana, 1974), p. 129.

the cycle of grace, namely bringing *significance* to his ministry and identity. In this regard he was able to declare, 'I am the way and the truth and the life . . .' (John 14:6), such language having all the overtones of divinity from the Old Testament revelation of God to Moses, 'I AM WHO I AM' (Exodus 3:14). Consequently, after his death and resurrection, Jesus was also able to claim 'all authority in heaven and on earth' (Matthew 28:18), and he passed that authority on to his disciples and their successors.

The fourth element in the cycle, *achievement*, is summed up in Jesus' declaration from the cross, 'It is finished' (John 19:30). This indicated that he had achieved what he had come to do by demonstrating his obedience to the Father, and this became the model for all disciples in all ages to imitate. By his death Jesus removed all the barriers that had previously prevented an intimate relationship with the Father. All believers are therefore recipients of the benefits of the victory Christ won for them, and he graciously and liberally bestows these benefits through the power of the Holy Spirit.

The humanistic and rational path is to reverse this process, reflecting the debilitating effects that the modern Western worldview has had on the ministry intended for the church. As I described earlier in the book, before my own encounter with the Holy Spirit through the teaching of John Wimber, my faith had become a form of legalistic religious consumerism. I now see that, subconsciously, my reasoning had followed this naturalistic path through my thirst for theological knowledge – in the hope that perhaps I could gain significance in circles that *seemed* to matter. Such an undertaking required a considerable amount of effort, because I felt there was so much I needed to learn. I had a mistaken belief that it would improve my feelings of self-worth, and it all had much more to do with religion than a living faith. The angst brought about by trying to reverse the cycle of grace which God gave me as a gift was largely removed when I realised that, as Paul says, 'It is by grace you have been saved, through faith – and this not from yourselves, it is the gift of God – not by works, so that no-one can boast' (Ephesians 2:8). To reverse the process means to create my own image of God, which is the height of folly and, indeed, idolatry.

The church and its members have no authority to coerce God into doing their will. Their only right is to seek to discern what God wants by using the gifts he has given, namely the Holy Spirit and the Bible, and to use them with the authority and purpose he intended. If Christians are to avoid being dictated to by the naturalistic values of their society, and if they are to avoid feelings of isolation, they need to develop what Scott Peck describes in his book *The Different Drum* as the new ethic of 'soft individualism'. Soft individualism teaches that people cannot truly be themselves until they are able to share freely the things they have in common. These things include weakness, incompleteness, imperfection, sin, lack of wholeness and self-sufficiency. What is needed is the kind of softness that enables believers to be like permeable membranes, allowing the grace of God to seep into them and the changes he causes to seep out, so that they might act as agents for good in the world.

7

Lifeskills for Doing Church

In many ways the church at large has become terribly complicated for its members. It seems that in order to do anything effectively and play a significant part in shaping its life, one has to go to a Bible college or theological institution to acquire the 'right' knowledge. For most members this leads to a high degree of dependence on already overworked leaders and trained clergy, who tell them what to do. Such a structure creates a membership that talks more *about* life in the church, rather than *living out* that life, using the resources given by the Holy Spirit for doing the business of the kingdom. Many church members hear preaching and sing songs that reflect the desire to see God's kingdom advanced here on earth as in heaven; many weep and pray fervently – yet church, even though it plays a major part in people's lives, is often subservient to the way their lives are lived in the home, leisure and work environments. It is just another segment in the round of activities that make up life.

In this chapter I would like to describe how St Thomas's has sought to reverse this trend, by using the Lifeskills course to help people understand the particular gifts God has given to the church, and to open their eyes to how they can function as individuals within the body, using the grace God has given them for their calling. Grace is given to each believer in the form of a call to be what God intends that person to be, namely one of the five types described in Ephesians 4:11. That call is then strengthened by the tools described in 1 Corinthians 12, and applied in the way set out in Romans 12.

Identifying all members as ministers

The Lifeskills course has different entry levels, depending on how new to the faith a person is, the level of their maturity, and the degree of responsibility involved in the role to which they have been called in the church. Course One is targeted at those at the entry level of discipleship, and generally follows induction through the Beta course. Course Two is designed for those who have responsibilities commensurate with leading a small group. Each course involves six sessions of approximately two hours each. The syllabus includes direct teaching incorporating an interactive format, as well as group discussion. A third course has been developed to cater for those who lead clusters and are engaged in church-planting, or those who will soon be doing so. This last is held once a month over a nine-month period and is more comprehensive than the other two courses. The material for each level is constantly under review to ensure that it remains relevant to the ongoing vision of the church.

The Lifeskills course material actually began as the syllabus for a leadership course organised by Mike Breen when he was the vicar at All Saints' Church in Brixton. After joining St

Thomas's, he taught the same principles initially to those already in leadership positions within the church. Over four years more than 200 people took part. In recognition of the fact that these principles were also applicable to the rank-and-file members, the name of the course was changed to Lifeskills to reflect its real content and character.

Geometric shapes are used as memory aids for the course's core principles, and five are currently used. These are under-pinned by appropriate biblical foundations, with particular concentration on those passages examined in Chapter 4. Quite simply, Lifeskills is designed to equip the believer for life. It forms the vocabulary that expresses the theology and practice of St Thomas's, providing a clear grid through which members can gain a greater understanding of what God intends to do in their personal lives and in the church. It also acts as a practical and interactive way of advancing through the process of being a disciple of Jesus Christ and discovering what it means to model oneself on him.

The design of each level encourages development and under-standing, as well as communicating the pilgrimage dimension of the faith. By looking at a different shape in each session (see below), participants gain insight into how they can learn from the experience of their Christian life to date, and how they might further develop the rhythm of that life, leading to greater balance in terms of UP, IN and OUT relationships. Each differ-ent stage of their development is considered, and this provides a framework they can use to mature any of the five aspects of ministry in the body set out in Ephesians 4. The final session looks at the range of biblical gifts available to disciples to enable them to grow in their ministry and in their relationships with God and fellow members of the body.

The learning circle

The first shape is described as the *learning circle* (shown below). It introduces participants to the principle of determining significant events in their lives, and learning the lessons from those events which ultimately move them closer to God's will. The circle is based on Jesus' declaration, "'The time [*kairos*] has come," he said. "The kingdom of God is near. Repent and believe the good news!'" (Mark 1:15). God's kingdom, in the form of *kairos* time, is constantly breaking into the lives of believers. The key is to recognise how often this happens and whether it leaves them the same or is an agent of change, making them into the likeness of Jesus through the process of repenting and believing, which is a constant in this ongoing cycle. If disciples are consistent in their walk, this should produce a cyclical forward movement like that of a spring.

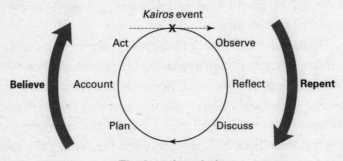

The learning circle

The first stage of repentance can be broken down into three components as God impacts the disciples' lives. First, they must *observe* what God is communicating through a particular event. Second, they *reflect* – consciously or unconsciously – on the nature and changes which the event suggests. Third, they *discuss* with others, or consider privately, the change or repentance needed in order to move forward. In this context, repentance may not involve a strictly moral action, but a more general change of attitude, behaviour or surrender of will – depending on what is actually taking place during the *kairos* experience.

On the other side of the circle, the three steps towards active trust and faith in God help believers to *plan* a new way forward in light of their act of repentance. *Being accountable* to a member of the body draws on the inherent strength which the body possesses through the grace of God. This, along with the 'discussion' dimension, is a key element of the IN aspect of small group life. The next logical step is to *act* – to move forward in one's faith by conforming more closely to God's will, using the lessons learned from the *kairos* event.

Alongside *kairos* time there is *chronos* time. The derivative word 'chronological' suggests an orderly sequence of events, often with no special significance attached, and is usually used in the context of dates or times. *Kairos*, by contrast, refers to an event or crisis where time seems to stand still, a period when *chronos* time is of little importance. It can be used of events or physical things which mark a significant shift in a person's life – rites of passage, the birth of a child, the effect of a sunset, a worship experience, an encounter with God's Holy Spirit, the death of a loved one. *Kairos* can be a positive or negative experience and, unlike *chronos*, is never neutral.

Once disciples recognise the importance of *kairos* and understand how God is constantly seeking to communicate his grace in order to bless and move them on to maturity, the ability to be alert in this regard becomes an essential means of developing their pilgrimage. We find that *kairos* comes in many forms, through personal devotions, small group life, clusters, celebrations, the workplace, and so on.

The object of using this methodology is to alert members' senses to God breaking into their lives, and to demonstrate the ongoing effect of the rule and reign of God at a personal as well as a corporate level. The notion of kingship emphasises the need to surrender to God's authority – but not in the sense usually applied to the geographical rule of an earthly king. In the case of God's rule, his reign is gracious and, through the interaction of his Holy Spirit, hovers over the Christian's present and future life. To that end, he uses all manner of events and circumstances.

Through this segment of the course, participants are alerted to the need to be open and sensitive to God's rule at all times, using the potential of *kairos* events at what appear to be times of 'crisis' in an individual's daily life. The more the surrender process is applied, the greater the blessing for the individuals involved – which in turn affects for good the life of the body to which they belong.

The rhythm of life

The second principle of discipleship addresses the importance of the *rhythm of life*, and is represented by a semicircle and pendulum (see below). Following on from the concept of *kairos*, it is designed to help disciples to understand that, in addition to breaking into their lives, God has designed humans for seasons of work and rest.

The lesson of the semicircle is based on the Old and New Testament teaching about the Sabbath. God created the heavens and the earth, its creatures, and lastly man and woman. He then rested and, by implication, so did they, before he committed them to his service. In humanist terms, rest is a necessity to combat the effects of hard work – it is an entitlement, a reward for application. God's intention runs counter to this, in that prior to the fall work and labour progressed out from resting in the relationship which God had created in the beginning. This idea is developed, in a broad sense, to enable those on the course to understand the concept of *action, reflection, being* and *doing*, as seen in God's action at creation as described in Genesis 1–3. The effects of the fall marred God's intention for humanity, but the coming of the kingdom was a sign that the broken relationship with the Father – and the resulting disruption of the Sabbath principle – has been restored.

The rhythm of life

An essential component of redemption is that a Christian should be healthy, and this means allowing the Holy Spirit to set the pace of life. He is the only one who can enable us to establish a healthy balance between work and rest on a daily, weekly, monthly and seasonal basis. Jesus describes this in John 15 as a time of abiding, growing, fruiting and pruning. The pace of modern life tends to blur our perspective, especially when it comes to managing our time according to the overall plan which God has for our lives. As discussed earlier, the cycle of grace incorporates a more reasoned biblical approach to this aspect of discipleship. Most people are caught up with what they *do* in life rather than who they *are*, and the pressure to strive towards that end is usually fairly high. There is no argument against the principle that the created order was for people to *do* things; from the perspective of Scripture the difficulty lies in the problems associated with building God's identity and values around those activities.

The aim at this point is to reinforce the concept that everything about a believer is defined by God, and each individual's task is to live in the truth of who he or she is in him. This draws on the role of the Holy Spirit as the 'Counsellor', as described by Jesus in John 14:16–17. The word 'paraclete' – meaning advocate or counsellor – can also be defined as 'pace-setter', someone getting alongside and setting the pace, directing a godly rhythm of life. Paul wrote, 'Let the peace of Christ rule in your hearts, since as members of one body you were called to peace. And be thankful' (Colossians 3:15). The Greek word for 'rule', *brabeno*, meaning to arbitrate or referee, is used to qualify the effect of that peace, and is therefore an important dimension of a disciple's lifestyle. It acts as a meter by which the tempo of life can be gauged for good or ill. Only God can channel this grace. It is not a human attribute, but divinely imparted, and as such is an important dimension in the decision-making process of discipleship.

A balanced Christian life

The third principle, depicted by the triangle shown below, addresses the need for a balanced Christian life which incorporates three dimensions referred to earlier in the book.

The upward dimension reflects the life and relationship of the disciple to God. Jesus' lifestyle was consistent and his principles lived out on a daily basis. He always ensured that he had sufficient time alone with his heavenly Father each day, often rising early before the disciples were awake and going to a quiet

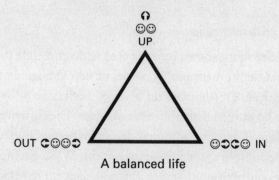

A balanced life

place to hear his daily instructions. In John 5:19, Jesus emphasised that he could do nothing by himself, and only did what he saw the Father doing. His disciples were so moved when they observed his lifestyle that they said, 'Lord, teach us to pray' (Luke 11:1). They recognised that the upward dimension was the source of all fruitfulness, and they wanted to have a similar relationship.

It is noteworthy that Jesus called together the Twelve after he had finished praying and after 'designating them apostles – *that they might be with him*' (Mark 3:13–14, italics mine). This underlines the need for healthy relationships with other believers in the body, the church – one aspect of the inward dimension. The verse goes on to add 'and that he might send them out to preach', indicating that there was also a requirement for them to have an outward relationship with the world and their environment.

The triangle emphasises the fact that all three elements are required to interrelate. They are not separate compartments in life. The triangle also illustrates how one element leads to another, in a combination of ways. The forum of a small group within the church seems to St Thomas's to be the best way of ensuring that all three elements are lived out as intended.

Phases of development

The square shape shown below is used to demonstrate the principle that there are invariably phases of development in the life of a disciple. This mirrors the style of leadership adopted by Jesus as he worked with his twelve disciples. The current culture of leading in many traditional denominational churches has developed into a system of management. While having many positive contributions to make, this management style lacks the dimension of leadership shown to be essential to church practice in the New Testament.

Leadership in the church is not a position; rather, it is how a Christian relates and behaves. For faith to operate effectively, it should be reflected in a Christian's lifestyle and act as a witness to those who do not believe (2 Corinthians 5:16–21). In a sense all Christians are leaders, though some have a higher profile than others. This is illustrated by the fact that most believers are models or mentors to others, at least in the sense of their example and lifestyle, without their even realising it. To continue with the analogy of the body, logic would dictate that leaders are called to lead the organism of the church, not necessarily its organisation.

This segment of the course therefore seeks to unpack the dynamics of leadership, at whatever level is applicable. Management is important, but it must be subservient to leadership in the biblical sense, and able to give format and clarity that allows mission to be prioritised, developed and maintained. In recognition of this, the square has been adapted from Kenneth Blanchard's *The One-Minute Manager*.[1]

---

[1] Kenneth Blanchard, *The One-Minute Manager* (HarperCollins, 1985), pp. 46–58.

Phases of development

In this shape four distinct phases of leadership are identified, all of which Jesus employed at different stages as he discipled the Twelve. The letter 'D' represents the disciple dynamic present during this process. The same principles can be applied by using 'L' for leadership, or 'M' for marriage.

D1 indicates the stage classified as the classical, directive style. When Jesus called the disciples, they were initially enthusiastic, in the light of who he was and what he had done, and they had confidence to follow him. While not fully understanding Jesus' purpose, they were happy to carry out any task he gave them. At this stage, because of their lack of experience and competence, Jesus was more directive in his leadership style. He was confident in what he was calling them to do, and because he only did what he saw the Father doing, he did not need to refer to anyone else. This included leading by example, demonstrated in his ministry as he went about preaching, healing and casting out demons, with little explanation given to those who witnessed him at work (Matthew 4:19; Mark 1:15–18; Luke 5:4–5).

D2 highlights the change that comes about when the first flush of enthusiasm fades, after someone has been called and chosen, when the reality of being a disciple takes root. For the first disciples, it involved coming to terms with opposition from the authorities, as well as rejection from the crowd who followed Jesus' ministry. This was compounded by the fact that they had left the security of their professions and family, and came at a time when they no doubt found their confidence and enthusiasm at a low ebb. At this point, Jesus encouraged them by describing the vision of what God was going to do with them, and his input was like that of a shepherd, offering the grace needed to help them move forward both in his ministry and their own (Luke 12:32–34).

D3 marks the point where Jesus leads them further along their pilgrimage by encouraging and developing their growing experience, competence and confidence. At this stage Jesus remains accessible, spending lots of time with the disciples, but acting in a much less directive fashion as they begin to play a greater part in decision-making (John 15:1–8). Jesus says of them, 'I no longer call you servants, because a servant does not know his master's business. Instead, I have called you friends, for everything that I learned from my Father I have made known to you' (John 15:15).

D4 represents the acceptance by Jesus of these followers to the extent that he delegates his authority to them so that they might operate with the same power he possesses (Matthew 28:18–20).

The experience of addressing the issues posed in this process gives the course participants greater confidence, providing a meaningful matrix for 'pressing towards their high calling in Christ Jesus'. Frequently, after the initial flush of D1 and having moved on to D2, people seek to return to the effects they experienced at the first stage. Someone, for example, may attend a supercharged conference or gathering where the expectation and ambience is on a different plane to that of normal church life. When they return to their local church, the atmosphere often does not reflect the excitement they have just left behind. The music, the quality of the speakers, the luxury of living in close proximity with other likeminded Christians, all seem so much of a contrast with the mundane experience of normal daily life. Understandably, many people rapidly lose the benefits they gained during that special time. Their response is to shut down the senses God has newly opened until a similar experience comes about, and by doing this they miss out on the richness and quality of moving through the stages of D3 and D4. They and the church body are impaired and crippled because of a failure to 'work out [their] salvation with fear and trembling' (Philippians 2:12).

A variant of this leadership paradigm can be summed up helpfully in the following way. D1 signifies Jesus saying to the disciples, 'I do; you watch.' In D2 he is saying, 'I do; you help.' In D3 he is telling them, 'You do; I help.' Finally, in D4 he says, 'You do; I watch.'

The five aspects of ministry

The fifth and final principle, represented by the pentagon below, involves the exploration of the five aspects of ministry as set out in Ephesians 4. The passage is unpacked as I described in Chapter 5, to show that everyone has strength in one of the five roles. All will grow in their gifting if the other core principles (represented by the geometric shapes shown above) are developed in the way they have learned. During the lifetime of a believer, growth often involves going through different phases and seasons which provide experience of all five ministries. During this session, we help participants understand how the five ministry roles function best in terms of the kingdom, and aim to enable each member within the body to recognise their worth and play their part in building up the whole body.

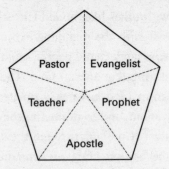

The five aspects of ministry

Determining members' ministry and gifts

Mission, in a church context, means the fulfilment of Christ's commission to his people and, as the body of Christ, those who make up the church's members are part of that. A human body has a skeleton structure that gives it shape and form, and it also has a means of digestion which allows the body to be fed, providing nourishment for its growth and development. A respiratory system enables it to inhale good air as well as exhale waste gases, and a nervous system forms the communication network, controlling how the body functions. As it is with a human body, so it is with members of the church, who are the sum of the whole body, with Christ as its head. Each member of the body therefore needs to understand the part for which he or she has been designed. As Paul says, 'For we are God's workmanship, created in Christ Jesus to do good works, which God *prepared in advance for us to do*' (Ephesians 2:10, italics mine).

Contrasting models

Under the Christendom model, which is the way the church has functioned for hundreds of years, the clergy have largely acted as 'omnicompetent priests', while members, for the most part, have been passive – one might almost say parasitical – and content to pay their leaders a salary for the privilege. In some cases the leadership has turned out to be strong, central and unquestioned, particularly in churches with an episcopal form of government, though similar models exist in some nonconformist traditions. This kind of high-status role, with its attendant authority, has in particular been the backbone of the church experienced by the Builder generation, who make up the majority of members in the traditional denominational churches. Such a model, however, has been rejected by their offspring, the Boomers, and it is now seen to be largely irrelevant to the Boomers' own children, the emerging Generation Xers. Currently, clergy are generally seen as those who oversee rites which are part of the lifestyle of those who regard the religious dimension as having some importance in their lives – including civic events where a token church presence is deemed to be valid, and such rites of passage as infant baptism, confirmation, marriage and burial of the dead. They may also provide a pastoral presence in people's lives at times of crisis.

All this is in marked contrast to the model envisaged by the writers of the New Testament. The church appears to be worked out in quite a different form in the Acts of the Apostles and the instructions given in the Epistles. Here, the work and person of the Holy Spirit has a wider implication than in the Christendom model. The Holy Spirit is described as stirring the God-conscious element in humankind into following a lifestyle that incorporates the whole nature of Christ, empowering believers in their inner lives and making them fully conscious of their God-given calling. Romans 8 elaborates on this, with Paul describing the Spirit as the one who gives life. His 'law' is the 'law of life' and to be 'led by the Spirit', to have the 'mind of the Spirit', is to live. This is not the preserve only of those who are ordained clergy, elders or deacons in the church – it is the inheritance of all who are 'in Christ'.

To allow Christ's Spirit to rule in this way is far more searching than the demands made by any traditional denominational structure and its officers. Such a perspective carries the promise of empowerment until Jesus comes again. Every Christian has this inheritance and is expected to let it be worked out to the full. The New Testament emphasises this aspect frequently, not only at a personal level but also within the whole body of the church. Leaders are not excluded: they must expect the church to function in this way, and it is vital that they exercise the anointing God has given them for their task, otherwise the resources of the kingdom will be squandered.

When New Testament principles are put into practice, members who make up the body become the expression of God's love and kindness, which is part of the salvation process. This reflects the self-giving of the Father, in whose heart lies true motivation for all things. God's mission, focusing on salvation through Christ, empowers believers to be Christ-like, and they are able to enter into God's own mission more fully, expressing his kindness and proclaiming the gospel to a world in need of salvation.

God's mission to his creation, focused on Jesus, lies at the heart of Paul's eloquent hymn of praise, in which he describes the church's response to Christ's commission set out in Ephesians 3:10 – namely that the church should fulfil the original purpose for his creation and make known 'the manifest wisdom of God'. What this boils down to, in practical terms, is serving and meeting our neighbours' needs as and when the opportunity arises, empowered with the gifts and abilities given by God through his Holy Spirit. Such an undertaking will be most effective when we have a clear understanding both of the particular gifts that God gives and of the opportunities that present themselves to the church in its ministry. If we each understand how we have been created and how we are designed to function, we can more easily appropriate the grace by which we have been called.

Identifying a base ministry

The experience of St Thomas's has been that those who follow the Lifeskills course take significant steps towards identifying their calling – or, in the church's vocabulary, their 'base ministry'. The course provides a process whereby they can determine with which of the five ministries in Ephesians 4 they most closely identify. This process includes an examination of the personality and characteristics of the types of people who make up society. Using this matrix, participants are better able to understand how God has redeemed the existing character and nature of people, and how he in turn deploys them within the body through their relationship with him and with each other. In this way he is able to compensate for the apparent weaknesses or shortfalls in any given group. The assumption from Scripture is that every group that meets as a church, with Christ as its head, possesses all it needs in order to minister God's grace effectively (1 Corinthians 1:7). It is God's self-giving initiative to the church, the gift of love and forgiveness in salvation, a gift that empowers and equips us to function in the way he wants.

Grace within the body comes in the form of a call to be one of the five sorts of person described in Ephesians 4:11 – an apostle, prophet, evangelist, pastor or teacher. Identification of these fivefold ministries is facilitated by an understanding of where members in the church find themselves on the continuum shown below. There are no hard-and-fast rules and the process used is a tool, not an end in itself. In general, however, apostles, prophets and evangelists tend to be of a more pioneering disposition, while teachers and pastors tend to prefer a settler role. There are undoubtedly pioneering pastors and non-pioneering prophets, but in general these distinctions hold true.

An understanding of how God has created a person for his service begins with consideration of the ways in which that person accomplishes a task, according to temperament. Are they extrovert or introvert? Initially this takes the form of examining the ways people engage with or are excited by a project or set of circumstances – and this is accorded a position on the 'pioneer/settler' continuum, from 1 to 10 (see diagram below). This is not a measure of anyone's lack or excess of confidence, but a description of how people live and process things in different ways. In society these temperaments are essential for life and growth, and the way they operate within the church should likewise be recognised. Used wisely, this process helps to determine people's base ministry from the perspective of Ephesians 4. A more refined questionnaire, using a Myers Briggs Type Indicator format, is set out in the appendix on pages 201–14 and, while not definitive, is arguably more accurate.

Phase ministries

St Thomas's contention is that each member in any church situation has a base ministry (i.e. apostle, prophet, evangelist, pastor or teacher), given by God for the lifetime of that

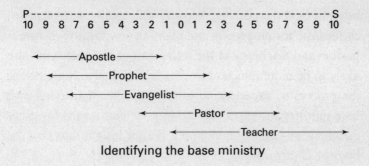

Identifying the base ministry

believer. From time to time, there are also periods in which a disciple will be called by God to function in another ministry for a phase. An evangelist, for example, may act for a time as a pastor, or an apostle as a teacher, and so on. This is particularly true for those in leadership positions, but discernment is needed. If we understand how we have been designed and gifted by God, we are less likely to misuse our energy or pursue a role that is not ours, and we will be better able to rest in Christ. A general guideline for recognising that a particular phase of gifting is coming to an end is often a lack of enthusiasm and energy for the task, which usually indicates a lack of grace to do that particular ministry.

All five ministries relate to and overlap with the others. Always there should be the sense of anointing and grace to fulfil the task, evidenced at a personal level as well as being affirmed by others within the body. Someone who is a pastor, for example, will generally encounter less stress in engaging in ministry at this level than someone who is an evangelist acting in that role. The former has a natural disposition towards that ministry, whereas an evangelist, while enjoying the social interchange, has a more natural desire to share the gospel with an unbeliever. Similarly, prophets seem better able to pray and listen to God than others. Apostles will usually have plenty of enthusiasm for pioneering and planting new ventures, whereas pastors and teachers – at the settler end of the spectrum – are likely to be more reluctant to pursue such paths. Nonetheless, the process of experiencing ministries other than one's own base ministry increases respect, honour and regard for other members, and helps to develop a greater insight into how the body of Christ works.

Anointing for ministry

At the end of the Lifeskills course, each participant is in a position to compile a personal 'Ministry Profile'. This helps them to focus on where it is that the Lord is currently calling them, according to the gifts with which he has equipped them. The profiles are then used to match up the human resources available within the body, in view of the needs and opportunities the Lord is currently presenting to the church. Such personal ministry identification is rewarding both for the individuals and for the church, as it helps to strengthen the whole body. People are able to focus more clearly and effectively on the areas of kingdom service into which God is calling and anointing them.

The liberty brought to members in this regard removes the blockages and hindrances that rob them of their identity in Christ. When evangelism becomes a priority in a church, for example, it is an immense relief for those whose base ministry is not evangelism that the other ministries receive equal recognition. They are not excluded from being effective witnesses, but the church body knows that their true responsibility lies elsewhere, perhaps in supporting and encouraging those who are evangelists. They are thus freed to direct their energies in the most effective way. This resonates with Paul's declaration, 'From him the whole body, joined and held together by every supporting ligament, grows and builds itself up in love, *as each part does its work*' (Ephesians 4:16, italics mine).

The appendix on pages 201–14 sets out the profile questionnaire currently in use at St Thomas's Church, following the Myers Briggs Type Indicator method. It is there as an indicator, a tool to help people better understand the calling that Jesus makes on their lives. Our experience has shown that, when used in this way, it is liberating and beneficial for individuals and the church as a whole. The results also provide small group and cluster leaders with invaluable information as they seek to identify and plan appropriate outward activities.

As will be described in the next chapter, this has enabled St Thomas's to be effective in mission to our community and city of Sheffield. It has not been accomplished without difficulty, but the journey has been worth the effort and brought rewards.

8

Doing Church at St Thomas's

A meeting of generations

St Thomas's strength thus far has been its ability to reach the emerging generation in a relevant way. Moreover, the church's strong leadership style is appreciated in a culture that lacks good role models. The differences between the Builder, Boomer and Buster generations were laid out in Chapter 3, but here I would like to say a little more about the approach St Thomas's has taken to the problem of communication and inclusion across the generations.

We have discovered that the Builder generation put a greater emphasis on behaviour, and that format and structure feature prominently in their concerns. This is often expressed in a desire for the use of 'right' liturgy and formal dress at worship, and in their attitude towards matters of finance.

Boomers, on the other hand, are more concerned with belief, particularly at a personal level. This is made more pronounced by the fact that many of them have been raised in a very individualistic lifestyle, and is often expressed by a need for their personal desires to be met by the church or other agencies, with the expectation that the 'service' provided should be of a high standard. Belonging and behaviour are of less significance for them.

In a further contrast, Busters place a greater priority on belonging, because of the fragmented background against which they were raised. To restore the balance, we recognise that behaviour and belief need to be restored to them using a mentoring approach, sharing with them the Builders' and Boomers' experience of life.

A whole-church emphasis

Our initial understanding of these different characteristics came through an accident of events in relation to St Thomas's mission (as described in Chapter 1). By January 1998, in order to create space for growth at the parish church and to serve our vision for the city, we decided to make use of some rented premises in the city centre on a weekly basis. Those members who regarded the community as their main mission priority were asked to attend worship at the parish church, and all others to worship at the rented leisure centre in the city. After the first three months of this experiment, we began to discern the process of doing church in a different way.

Despite meeting at two sites, our intention was always to ensure that there was a whole-church perspective. This accorded with the intentions expressed at the formation of the LEP, namely to have all things in common and to celebrate the differences of emphasis while maintaining the same vision and values. The vision was to equip each generation to meet their peers with the gospel and live the lifestyle of the kingdom, using the values of God's grace under the covenant God has made with his people. The concepts of UP, IN and OUT form the umbrella structure for this vision and its values.

Such an approach is, in many ways, contrary to the traditional church's way of operating. In the excellent book *The Missional Church*, the chapter offered by Alan Roxburgh advocates a move to the sort of model used at St Thomas's. His interpretation of Ephesians 4:11, however, follows the usual Christendom line, seeing the five orders of ministry as referring only to leaders within the church.[1] St Thomas's, by contrast, understands the emphasis in the passage to be on all those who make up the membership of the church, not just the leaders. The passage makes no reference to gender, status or authority. Verse 7 says clearly, 'But to each one of us [i.e. all members of the church] grace has been given as Christ apportioned it,' and verse 11 goes on to describe how those gifts of grace are distributed throughout the whole body. Grace is not the preserve of leadership alone, but the inheritance of all members. For the most part, Roxburgh advocates such a concept, but he is still bound by the institutional interpretation of the passage.

The corporate, Spirit-empowered leadership described in Ephesians transcends clergy-laity difference. In the missional community all are ordained to ministry in their baptism; all receive the same vocation to mission; and all are gifted in various ways for that mission as they participate in the twofold journey of the reign of God that is both inward and outward. Overcoming the professional

---

[1] Alan J. Roxburgh, 'Missional Leadership: Equipping God's People for Mission' in *The Missional Church*, ed. Darrell L. Guder (Eerdmans, 1998), p. 199.

clergy-shaped leadership models is an essential shift towards a missional leadership.[2]

Involving the whole membership, St Thomas's uses the concepts of UP, IN and OUT as a means of achieving community, and this has been proved to operate well at both a personal and a corporate level. The primary unit is the small group, and this model helps to release members to determine the emphasis of their ministry. If a member's relationship with God is lacking, the UP aspect is a means of addressing that deficiency. If relationships are affected by illness, whether emotional or spiritual, this can also be addressed within the small group using the IN aspect, which also offers an opportunity to have fun and relax on trips to the cinema, the theatre, and so on. The OUT aspect dictates mission emphasis and ranges from comparatively high-profile projects involving work with homeless people and drug addicts, to Radical Pursuits (which is offering an act of service to individuals and communities, with no strings attached) and other servant evangelistic projects, and acting as serious intercessors for particular situations as part of extending the kingdom of God.

This structure is lightweight and low maintenance, in order to allow the leadership to attend to the development of the vision and the direction of the church's ministry as a whole. If an inordinate amount of resources are needed to maintain a project, or if its vision is unclear, it usually means that it is too costly to be resourced by the people and equipment available, and those who service it soon lose their 'grace' to continue.

We use the diagram shown below to depict the way the church

---

[2] *Ibid.*, p. 200.

operates, basing the structure on the foundational blocks of our vision and values. The vision is updated and our values restated on Vision Sunday, which is held annually in late September or early October.

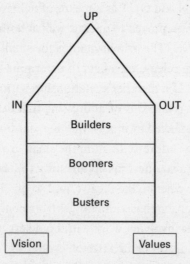

The operational structure of St Thomas's

St Thomas's recognises that there are defects in all attempts to make the church relevant and geared up for mission. History attests that no one model prevails. It is easy to see contradictions in the past and to accuse ecclesiastical structures of being more concerned with maintaining their own presence than with conducting any outward mission. Nonetheless, our desire, in following the model we do, is not to unchurch others, but rather to recognise more widely that God is at work in all cultures, including the traditional denominations, and we need always to listen to the plans and purposes the Lord of the church has for its growth and development. With this in mind, we believe that considering the different generations as specific people groups, and including youth and children's work in a similar way, enables those working to win them into the kingdom to be clear about their approach and the resources they need. This, surely, can only make their mission more effective.

Small groups as a primary unit

The emerging generation recognise the cultural decay that has impinged on their lives and culture, but social agencies (including the church), however well intentioned they may be, seem unable to address their dilemma effectively. Postmodern culture is wary of glib explanations and a message that is too simplistic, because such palliatives do not engage with its pain. Generation Xers' worldview is formed by education, television, the internet and music. Most have no idea of what takes place inside church buildings. Their view of the Christian religion is mostly formed through media portrayals such as *Father Ted*, *The Vicar of Dibley*, the vicar in *Dad's Army*, and so on, which tend to suggest that the church is hollow and has little bearing on the real issues of life.

Some would see this emerging postmodern generation as unreachable. At St Thomas's, however, our desire is to emulate Darrell L. Guder's view:

> Missional communities of hospitality do not seek the homogeneous oneness hoped for by modernity, nor do they celebrate the fragmented diversity of post-modernity. They welcome and nurture the incredible richness and particularity of perspectives, backgrounds, and gifts but always within the embrace of God's reconciling unity.[3]

---

[3] Darrell L. Guder, *Missional Communities* (Eerdmans, 1998), p. 179.

Those who make up Generation X want, above all, to belong. When converted, they recognise that the relationship between God and themselves as worshippers is available as well. They become totally committed to a church using such a baseline because it reinforces that much desired sense of belonging. The maxim of 1 Chronicles 12:32, concerning the 'men of Issachar, who understood the times and knew what Israel should do', demonstrates how the unchanging message of the gospel is relevant to whatever era the church is called to serve.

Evangelism through relationships

With this in mind, part of the OUT process is to help all members, regardless of where they feature on the generational chart, to use their existing relationships as a means of inviting others to their small groups. This will also reflect confidence in the message of the gospel, which has the power to change those whom God brings into their orbit. The early church used similar methods, and the gospel spread mainly through 'informal missionaries' in the marketplace. Ordinary people, using existing formal and informal links, are encouraged to look for the action of the Spirit in the lives of the people around them – in the same way that Jesus looked and did only what he saw the Father doing.

As members concentrate on developing meaningful relationships with their peers, progress is made when these are viewed in terms of the theology of grace, and in particular what is called prevenient or anticipating grace. This describes the special work of the Spirit of God, who creates in the human heart the desire to be reconciled to God and to do his will. To be effective, the co-operation of believers is necessary at each phase of the preparation, but the function of this doctrine in

terms of witness and evangelism is often overlooked and underestimated. Thus if a believer is constantly open to the prompt-
ing of the Holy Spirit in their life, they will recognise the grace
of God working on a person who is on the edge of entering the
kingdom of God. Darius Salter's definition is helpful in understanding what takes place:

> Prevenient grace is the source of the soul's first spiritual stirrings
> and hunger for God. Prevenient grace differs from common grace
> in that the former is the dynamic intention of God to save mankind.
> The latter allows the world and its inhabitants to continue in exis-
> tence.[4]

An example of the outworking of this principle is found in
Luke 10. Jesus commissions 72 anonymous disciples to perform
the same task and mission that he gave the Twelve. In particular he instructs them, 'When you enter a house, first say, "Peace
to this house." If a man of peace is there . . . Stay in that house'
(Luke 10:5–7). A 'man [or person] of peace' is one on whom the
Spirit of God already rests, where the effect of prevenient grace
is evident. The text also suggests that a relationship may already
exist, or at least the potential for furthering the process of
grace.

John Charles Ryle, in his commentary *Expository Thoughts
on the Gospels, St Luke Volume 1*, describes a 'man of peace' as
one 'deserving your good wishes'.[5] Matthew Henry says that

---

[4] Darius Salter, *American Evangelism: Its Theory and Practice* (Baker, 1996),
p. 49.

[5] John Charles Ryle, *Expository Thoughts on the Gospels, St Luke Volume 1*
(William Hunt & Company, 1884), p. 351.

these are people whose 'hearts are as soft as wax to receive the impressions of divine grace. They are qualified to receive the comforts of the Gospel.'[6] Simeon, in the temple, was one 'awaiting the consolation of Israel' (Luke 2:25) and demonstrated the spirit of expectation that exists in the human heart, where the Holy Spirit is active prior to a revelation. The dynamic behind the 'person of peace' concept is the Holy Spirit, who directs disciples towards people on whom he is already working, and leads them to play the role predestined for them in the process of bringing other people to faith and continuing their spiritual growth. In this regard, members of St Thomas's are exhorted to look at those with whom they are already in relationship, be that at work or in other areas of their lives.

The emerging generation have a greater openness to things spiritual, and when coupled with social systems of common kinship, it seems community and interests are spheres of influence in which prevenient grace is easily recognised. Traditional churches still frequently use high-profile events which the public are invited to attend in the hope that they will make some form of commitment. This, however, is a modern model of evangelism. It does not make use of everyday relationships, as described above, and it certainly does not resonate with the postmodern culture. The marketplace – in which work, leisure and socialising take place – is a more obvious and productive place to target, and such an approach requires an expectation that the *culture* these people inhabit is capable of being redeemed as well.

---

[6] Matthew Henry, *Commentary on the Whole Bible, Matthew–John* (MacDonald Publishing Company), p. 681.

This 'anthropological' route has proved to be a rewarding one for St Thomas's to follow. One example among many of the usefulness of this approach is the story of one of our members who worked at a homeless shelter in the city and shared her night shifts with another girl. Over a period of weeks, during the quiet hours of the night, their conversation included discussion about Christianity. Our member recognised that her colleague was a person of peace, and she invited her to attend the Easter evening celebration at St Thomas's. The whole experience of that evening, the powerful presence of the Holy Spirit and the astonishing discovery that God could be so real in a church service, resulted in the girl dissolving into floods of tears and later making a profession of faith in Jesus.

Clusters, celebrations and the parish church

Small groups may be the primary unit through which St Thomas's works out its kingdom principles of UP, IN and OUT, but regular attendance at cluster meetings and celebration events are also essential components in the process (see discussion in Chapter 1). There is also the option of attending the parish church in Crookes, where the emphasis is on outreach to the community through social action, servant evangelism and planting out clusters that meet in schools and other suitable premises.

Worshippers at the parish church are mainly those of the Builder generation or with that approach, although a large number of young families attend as well. Along with their work of outreach to the community, the older members are seen as an essential building block in the wider church, especially with reference to the Buster generation. Part of our vision is to release and equip them to be mentors, rather like grandparents, to the wider church family. Those of the older generation are the only credible eyewitnesses to a time and a culture that possessed a quality community life, with attendant meaningful relationships – something which is lacking in the emerging generation. Those with good Christian life experience, who are able to bridge the generational gap by coming to terms with the values of postmodernism without feeling threatened, are introduced to members of the younger generation, in the hope that the befriending process will draw those younger people into the church community.

The role of music in the life of the church

An important dimension of the celebration events is music, which is regarded as a particularly potent reference point for communicating the gospel, as well as enabling believers to worship, both personally and corporately. This aspect seems especially important for Boomers and Xers. In the 1960s, when Boomers were adolescents, the social, political, moral and global alienation they felt coincided with the rise of rock'n'roll music. The impact of this new genre was felt throughout the Western world.

> In early rock'n'roll . . . we have a medium with no message distinguishable from the medium itself. It was the medium which was anti-social, irreverent, and a threat to the dominant culture. In this regard rock'n'roll as a new, powerful and still developing medium was like an empty vessel waiting to be filled.[7]

---

[7] Roy Anker, *Dancing in the Dark* (Bridgepoint, 1991), p. 7.

The Boomer culture

This was the first time that the received wisdom of a former generation was rejected wholesale by their children. Authority, which in the past had been seen as a cherished inheritance in which government could be trusted and family, religion and the rule of law were stabilising forces, now became open to ridicule. A new way forward was sought, and music turned out to be a unifying dimension in this liberation from the oppression of adult culture.

A rugged individualism arose which urged this liberation concept on to an unprecedented level of hedonism, as people hoped to recapture a special, even holy dimension which they believed could not be found in the culture, values and religion of their parents. There was a desire for a new community, but it was hard to be a community when everyone had their own concept of what it should look like. As time passed, that dream was seen to be an illusion, and its dreams and ideals came to nothing. Boomers now have adult children, and in some cases grandchildren. As Anker says, 'Instead of expanding their consciousness, most of them worry more about receding hairlines, sagging bustlines, and expanding waistlines.'[8]

The Busters' world

The emerging generation now have MTV and digital music that can be downloaded from the internet, and unlike rock'n'roll its impact is not confined only to the Western world. The Busters' world is affected by a bombardment of unrelated information

---

[8] *Ibid.*, p. 213.

from a huge and global variety of sources. Electronic communications and technology bridge cultures on a scale their parents could never conceive. Referring to music in this context, Anker comments:

> The marvels of modern communications technology allow teenagers to participate in the same entertainment rituals as millions of other teens, even though they are separated from them by geography and cultural tradition. In the process, these countless others have become citizens in a new, commercially prescribed electronic culture.[9]

Listening to the same music, living the philosophy, knowing the bands, the singers and the lyrics are all compulsions which have significantly permeated the lifestyle of Generation Xers. Nightclubs and rave events are their habitat, their place of 'belonging'. Music styles such as techno, trance and garage access their heart language and affect their dress, lifestyle, friendship groups, alcohol preference and buying patterns. The ambience created at the events they attend declares their ownership of the space they inhabit and who they are. Video screens project the musicians with a close-up clarity that makes them seem more personable, and costumes and choreography serve to accentuate the experience. Digital technology produces near-perfect sound.

The wider availability of drugs adds another dimension. James F. Harris describes this commonplace aspect of the culture:

> One of the most dramatic subjective effects of taking some drugs is the increased importance of the present instant. With some drug

---

[9] *Ibid.*, p. 47.

experiences, time appears to be slowed to the point that the present moment seems to be extended indefinitely.[10]

The ability to alter one's state of mind in this way, and indeed one's entire personality and character, is so completely absorbing that it produces an even greater transrational feeling in which the experience becomes the dominant feature.

The rhythm and beat, the simple lyrics, the apparent freedom of spirit, are all compelling factors in the Generation X culture. Anker comments:

One understanding of art looks at popular entertainment as supplying consumers with an imaginative realm of refraction of life that contains clues, signs, and routes for interpreting the tangled welter of experience that life presents. Mythic narratives – whether they be Odysseus, Abraham Lincoln, or Rambo – tell us much about what the world might be like and how we should behave in it.[11]

Nonetheless, these elements, which provide such an apparently powerful experience, only heighten the inability of the culture and the artistic expression of its values to deliver satisfactory answers to the searching and longing of the human soul. This is particularly so for Busters, who experience the greatest sense of loss. The events become a means of escape into a world that seems to understand their dilemma, and where they can participate and celebrate the ethos itself: it is, in effect, a worship experience. A band with the ironic name of Faithless intone in

---

[10] James F. Harris, *Philosophy at 33 1/3 rpm* (Open Court, 1993), p. 127.

[11] *Ibid.*, p. 265.

their song 'God is a DJ' the lyrics 'This is my church / This is where I heal my hurts / And tonight God is a DJ.'

A question of worship

It is little wonder, then, that Generation Xers are not much engaged in traditional church worship, because the music and the way it is offered in most church settings is in such marked contrast to what Xers experience in their own world. Marva Dawn's preference is one which represents the approach of most church services, which are mainly in the hands of the Builder generation:

> I'd rather have no applause in worship than a failure to recognise that all congregants offer their best – serving on the altar guild, sweeping the carpet, making a banner, singing the liturgy with gusto, listening closely to sermons, reading well, and taking old bulletins out of hymnbooks.[12]

In the context of public worship, the assumption is that God is to be found among those worshipping, demonstrating his grace as well as responding to their actions. Some traditions, such as those represented by Marva Dawn, are so structured by fixed liturgy that there is little room for the spontaneity and side effects which are the norm in the contemporary secular music scene. As we saw in an earlier chapter, the liturgy for Holy Communion in the Anglican tradition begins with the celebrant saying, 'The Lord is here.' The worshippers respond, 'His Spirit is with us.' The language assumes interaction between the

---

[12] Marva J. Dawn, *Reaching Out Without Dumbing Down* (Eerdmans, 1995), p. 157.

worshippers and God, but in many cases it seems that the worshippers do not understand this or expect to be recipients of the grace God intends to impart through Holy Communion. Such confusion results from liturgy that has a format and language which are inaccessible. The New Testament describes the Holy Spirit as being 'manifested' with accompanying gifts – grace which he dispenses when the people of God gather to worship (1 Corinthians 12–14). Worship, in all its components, is a means of availing ourselves of that grace, and music plays a major part in the process of making such an experience accessible.

If secular and ungodly musicians can make their hearers believe the lyrics they sing by the ambience they create, which lacks the supernatural dimension the church has at its disposal, something is amiss if the church cannot do the same. Secular music seeks to meet the needs of its customers so that they can enjoy the experience, take pleasure in escaping the pressures of life and interact with the musicians. The concert organisers make a profit, the punters are happy, and so are the musicians. The Christian church has all the resources of heaven at its disposal when it gathers for worship, and surely it should be able to present a more dynamic ambience than any secular gathering can generate. Among the varied forms of church service, and where there are appropriate resources, there is arguably room for a concert model of worship.

The St Thomas approach

The intent of worship is to glorify God, which in turn has the effect of changing the lives of the participants. God hears his people confess their sins, and dispenses forgiveness on the basis of repentance. Intercession for the needs of the world gives a heavenly perspective on current issues. Healing, whether emotional or physical, takes place when the name of Jesus is invoked. The use of music and accompanying songs becomes the heart cry of the worshippers. Those who need to have an intimate relationship with the heavenly Father are converted.

These ideas are central to the way worship is viewed at St Thomas's, relevant to all who gather for worship, especially at celebrations. Sally Morgenthaler describes our situation well:

> Just how does evangelism take place in a service that is 'fully worship'? It happens in two ways: first, as unbelievers hear the truth about God (through worship songs, prayers, Communion, baptism, Scripture, testimonies, dramas, and so on); and second – more importantly – as they observe the real relationship between worshippers and God.[13]

In particular, observation of the relationship between worshipper and God becomes a powerful sign to a culture where people are desperate to belong and be accepted. Often in celebration worship the interaction is so strong and the power of the Holy Spirit so evident that people break down in tears, sway and dance to the music, become passionate as they sing the lyrics, physically shake with the effect of the Spirit, or sing in harmony in tongues.

Vineyard Ministries have had such an impact on St Thomas's because, as Donald E. Miller notes, they have helped through their music to 'democratise the sacred',[14] drawing on

---

[13] Sally Morgenthaler, *Worship Evangelism* (Zondervan, 1995), p. 88.

[14] Donald E. Miller, *Reinventing American Protestantism* (University of California Press, 1999), p. 80.

populist styles which 'symbolise a break with the old mores and provide a source of cohesion for those choosing the new way'.[15] Instead of singing the songs that express the experience of generations past – i.e. traditional hymns – the music and lyrics are contemporary and reflect the experience of the current generation.

This is not simply pandering to change and trend. Such an approach mirrors the methodology of leaders like Wesley and Booth, who took the popular tunes of their day and penned lyrics to go with them which reflected the experiences of the converts of their ministry. In effect, they were the disc jockeys of their era, and they had as many critics as current Christian songwriters do. The theology and majesty of Wesley's and Booth's hymns and musical style are not in question – it is simply that their language, for the most part, is alien to today's postmodern culture. If God inhabits the praises of his people (see Psalm 22:3), then the lyrics and musical styles used in worship should surely reflect the senses and experiences of the prevailing culture.

The way in which the secular world uses music as a form of worship – letting go, allowing the power of the music to bring feelings of enjoyment, and experiencing the sensory pleasure of sound and movement – may seem for some moderns to be a theological bridge too far. However, the church cannot ignore the experience of those who frequent venues where secular music is their heart language. John Fiske describes this experience vividly: 'The orgasmic pleasure of the body out of control – the loss of self – is a pleasure of evasion, of escape from the

---

[15] *Ibid.*, p. 81.

self-control/social-control by which in Foucault's telling phrase, "men govern themselves and others".'[16]

St Thomas's and its worshippers seek to use music in a way that is unafraid of letting go and allowing the power of God, their Creator and Redeemer, to bring forth an answering response to the witness of his Spirit within them. The assurance of God's presence in such circumstances allays any fears worshippers have of not being in control, because, by virtue of his nature, God transcends rational thought and human plans with his wisdom and purpose.

This is not without its problems for those leading celebrations. Spontaneity suggests an absence of structure, unexpected activity, and even lack of order and discipline. Yet unless there is space within the liturgy – whether 'fixed' or 'free' – for a response from the assembled worshippers, it amounts to a loss of authenticity in terms of worship. An encounter with the transcendent God demands a certain magnitude and flexibility of space in a psychological sense, because it is impossible to control an unmanageable God. Just as musicians and singers require a certain physical air mass to develop mass resonance, so worshippers need to have a similar freedom. The exercise of the charismata in this way thus places a high degree of responsibility on the worship leader or moderator, and is dependent on their willingness to seek and appropriate the benefits of all that is available from the grace of God within the worship experience.

In this regard, St Thomas's considers it to be of prime importance that a leader of a worship team should have a good relationship with God (UP), which is recognised as such by the

---

[16] John Fiske, *Understanding Popular Culture* (Rootledge Chapman Hall, 1989), p. 50.

senior staff and attested to by the rest of the church (IN), as well
as the technical ability to lead the worship (OUT). Musical
expertise is not enough to warrant such a responsibility – identity, intimacy and ability to worship through music must all be
evident from the three-dimensional foundations mentioned
above. From this baseline, spontaneity and openness to the
leading of the Holy Spirit, as well as the freedom to lead, are
all facilitated in an appropriate fashion for the celebration
events.

Critics argue from Paul's injunction in 1 Corinthians 14:40
that 'everything should be done in a *fitting and orderly* way',
whereas the emphasis at St Thomas's is that '*everything should
be done* in a fitting and orderly way' (all italics mine). For the
most part, the institutional church uses the former as a means
of exercising control and power to preserve the status quo. This,
however, fails to recognise the incredible redeeming features of
the culture found in the everyday experience of the emerging
generation, who regularly use all the emotions and senses in
their music and dance. Scriptural guidelines, which are timeless
and therefore also applicable to the twenty-first century, must
always be applied in the way James Dunn describes, commenting on Paul's words concerning the exercise of the charismata
in the Corinthian church:

> Paul is a charismatic who regards charis as fundamental to
> Christian living and experience of charisma as fundamental to the
> Christian community, but who sets his face against enthusiasm by
> insisting that all charismata must be tested, and only that charisma
> which manifests the grace of God is welcome.[17]

---

[17] James Dunn, *Unity and Diversity in the New Testament* (SCM, 1977), p. 195.

This is the litmus test for the leadership at St Thomas's whenever worship takes place.

Leadership issues

At St Thomas's we recognise that leaders at all levels need to be receptive enough to receive correction, as well as giving clear direction to others. To this end, accountability features high on the agenda and is usually included in all staff meetings. Using the UP, IN and OUT principles helps leaders to develop a high tolerance towards criticism and failure, and to accept affirmation without falling into the danger of pride. Risks can thus be taken without the fear of condemnation for apparent ineffectiveness and failure, and a leader's creativity can be given full rein, helping to develop integrity and character in a constructive way.

Leaders acting in this way help as a counterpoint for those they lead, supported by a consistent development of the spiritual disciplines in their personal life. Whether they are single, married or have families, they should reflect healthy relationships, recognisable particularly when they are under pressure – from within the church as well as without.

Flexibility to changes in structure pertinent to the ongoing vision of the church is also an essential quality. The bulk of the membership from whom leaders are chosen are of the postmodern generation, and it is necessary for them consciously to develop a tolerance towards the institutional aspects of denominational structures. The traditional model of leadership has always advocated a relatively formal style of training, usually through a theological college or seminary. Best results, however, are always obtained when those in leadership have first gained experience in the area for which they have an anointing, and then undergo training to back up that experience. Motivation to learn tends to be higher when people realise what they need to know in order to function better in their particular field.

There are four levels of organised leadership and relationship within the life of St Thomas's – namely small groups, clusters, celebration and accountability groups. These form the backbone of the body and are the framework around which everything else operates. As mentioned earlier, this is a low-maintenance structure that enables the leadership to attend to the vision and direction of the church's ministry, while employing effectively the biblical principle of equipping all the saints for the work of ministry.

Against the background of the Alpha and Beta courses, incorporation into St Thomas's includes three aspects. First, because of the fragmented nature of the converts' pasts, there needs to be an appraisal of what their lives were really like, conducted in an environment in which they will be heard without being condemned. Wherever possible, an accountability group of two or three other Christians of the same gender enables them to deal effectively with their past. This is in most demand from the emerging generation. If it is to be done properly, transparency in all aspects of life is recommended, including morality, habits, addictions, abuse and dysfunctional family backgrounds. The intention is to foster the change the Holy Spirit has already begun in their lives, to give them a greater freedom to move on to a blameless lifestyle. The backgrounds of most converts reveal a lack of this form of intimacy.

Second, all new members are also placed in a small group of 10–12 people. Those in the accountability group are usually members of the same small group. In the context of these small groups, UP, IN and OUT values are developed as being normative for members of St Thomas's.

Third, the small group is part of a cluster, which increases the circle of people to whom group members can relate in a meaningful way. Some of the emerging generation have chosen names for their clusters taken from their own particular worldview. One goes under the banner of 'Wac(ky) Racers' after the 1970s cartoon series. Their small groups are named after the characters of the series, e.g. Mutley, The Zippy Mississippi Racers, The Super Silly Swamp Sprinters, and so on. The cluster name begins with an acrostic of 'Wild Attractive Community' – to reflect their intended target group and the OUT dimension, and to make it sound like an attractive community that is worth belonging to. In the three years since its formation it has spawned a further three clusters. Quirky choices of names are by no means the preserve of Generation Xers: at the parish church there is one called .Com, indicating that they are also 'Church on Monday'. Another, called The Far Side, indicates their geographical location.

The devolved leadership of clusters, with its attendant accountability, offers opportunity for creativity at the widest level. The Lifeskills course gives members authority to make strategic and tactical decisions appropriate to their UP, IN and OUT activities. They are expected to pastor, share resources, identify gifting and enjoy God. This involves Bible study, ministry to one another's needs, social events and sports, including five soccer teams that play with other league teams in the region.

This aspect reinforces the concept of being proud of belonging and living by the new standards of the kingdom lifestyle.

Jerome H. Neyrey describes such a belonging dimension as being equivalent to a household in the Ancient Near East. In effect, the way the early church formed itself, reflecting strong relationships, was what made it attractive to converts of all social backgrounds: it seemed like something worth belonging to:

> The household, once the gathering place of the powerless and the marginalised, eventually emerges as the institution where God's spirit is truly active and where familial relations, shared resources, and communal values concretise the vision of a salvation to all the families of the earth.[18]

Many small groups have developed into what could be described as an 'extended household', a family unit that shares lives, walking into each other's homes without knocking, eating together and supporting each other. Particularly among the younger members, they have become places of trust and openness, a meaningful community, a belonging place, that is vibrant, fun and attractive to others.

---

[18] Jerome H. Neyrey, *The Social World of Luke–Acts* (Hendrickson Publishers, 1991), p. 217.

9

Representing the Reign of God

Some years ago I was invited to preach at a church on the out-skirts of Sheffield. They were about to use the Alpha course for the first time and wanted some advice on how to persuade people to attend. They already knew about our emphasis on the 'person of peace' and were anxious to know how they could apply it in this instance. During the sermon I described a person of peace as someone who felt at ease with Christians, in spite of them being 'a bit religious'. Examples might be people at work, neigh-bours, or the person you sat next to on the bus. I asked the 45 people present to raise their hands if they were able to identify such a person. About 35 responded and I advised them to invite the people they had identified to the Alpha course. In the end over 50 people turned up! It was not the power of the message I preached which made the difference; rather, it was the simple, practical outworking of kingdom principles that gave those church members boldness and courage.

Similar practical expressions of kingdom theology used at St Thomas's have been proved to be effective tools for growth and evangelism, because they help to solve what appear to be difficulties and fears about sharing the faith. Initially the task may appear daunting, but we can take encouragement from the New Testament. Early Christians faced similar problems, but they used their everyday situations as windows of opportunity to spread the gospel.

The model for growth used at St Thomas's is organic rather than programme orientated, and in some cases could have major implications for current leadership and authority structures in churches at a local level as well as at denominational level. In this chapter I include discussion of some of the issues related to integrating and monitoring such a process, to ensure that appropriate accountability procedures are in place to counter any danger of the abuse of power and privilege. Our experience at St Thomas's is that the use of such a model has facilitated considerable growth, particularly among the unchurched emerging generation.

A new authority structure

As part of St Thomas's aim to make headway into the current culture, we have implemented changes to the traditional church leadership structure. As indicated in the diagrams below, we follow neither the traditional Anglican hierarchical model, nor the traditional Baptist congregational style. Instead, the leadership provides the vision and general direction of the church, without necessarily forcing change or a particular pattern on any individual small group or cluster. In this way, members are encouraged to discern what God is saying specifically to them, and to follow his guidance accordingly. Any individual who has completed the Lifeskills course can start a small group with any focus, within the accountability structure of an existing cluster.

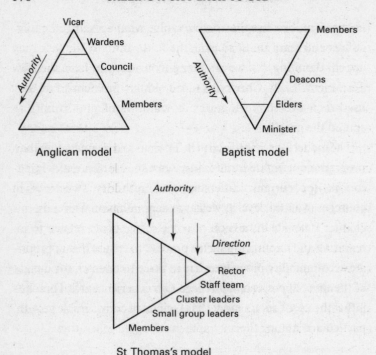

Anglican model

Baptist model

St Thomas's model

The staff operate as keepers of the vision, and regularly monitor the life of the clusters and small groups. Under this authority model, leaders are also expected to be visionary and give clear direction, under the guidance of the Holy Spirit. Mike Breen and I, as Associate Team Leader and Director of Mission respectively, head up other senior leaders, known as the Central Team, which includes the Financial Director and an Anglican vicar and his wife, who have oversight of training and development. Another Anglican vicar has oversight of the celebrations at the parish church (celebrations are gatherings of 200 or more people). An assistant Baptist minister heads up the morning city celebration. Other staff members, not ordained, lead celebrations or work among young adults and students in the inner city and the workplace.

Staff operating on the next level of leadership have specific responsibilities for other areas of our whole-church work. They are also mentored with a view to them becoming the next generation of senior leaders, succeeding the current central leadership team as the church grows in size and influence. They currently include a youth leader responsible for developing work in the community and the city, and a children's leader who works in a similar way, as well as being involved with cluster-planting. Other staff members include two Anglican curates, one acting as assistant for the parish church, the other as a researcher on the biblical process of the church's development. We also employ a worship director and various administrative staff and personal assistants. There are a total of 39 people employed by the church.

An elected church council has been put in place to ensure that the leaders do not become too autocratic in the discharge of their responsibilities. Part of the council's role is to help in assessing and processing the vision of the church and its out-working, while ensuring that relevant checks and balances are in place as deemed appropriate from the denominational perspectives. The council is made up of ex-officio (clergy) members and representatives from each of the clusters. Each member serves for a maximum term of three years. The council meets ten times a year and a full church meeting takes place once a quarter, which gives the senior leadership a chance to communicate and update the church's vision directly to the members. The full meeting also provides an opportunity to pray through issues affecting specific outreaches and ministries of the church.

Transition from bureaucracy to personal responsibility

St Thomas's has put mechanisms in place which are deliberately designed to enable members to give their personal responsibility full rein. The aim is to foster a sense of being a vital part of the body of the church and not a subject of a bureaucratic organisation. By encouraging application of the UP, IN and OUT principles, those who have the anointing are given the freedom to exploit their potential. When an opportunity is identified as part of the OUT dimension, for example, those involved gather others from among the membership – usually, but not exclusively, from their small group or cluster – to pray the idea through and apply the IN principles as taught on the Lifeskills course. The success and progress of these prayers and discussions determine whether the anointing of God is on the venture, thus fulfilling the third dimension of UP. Sometimes the ventures do not fulfil the criteria, but nothing is wasted and even the discarded ideas are considered effective in that they offer experience of discerning God's will in a given situation.

Such a method avoids lengthy discussion at senior staff level, and it allows the body to use the grace given to each member as described in Romans 12, 1 Corinthians 12 and Ephesians 4. In most instances, therefore, this form of growth allows the development of leadership potential among the members. In some cases individuals or groups are approached directly by staff members to pursue fresh opportunities not associated with small group and cluster activities, but such ventures are still explored using the UP, IN and OUT principles.

As mentioned above, those coming to faith are encouraged to undertake an honest appraisal of their past lives in the supportive context of a small accountability group. At its most effective, this fosters the changes the Holy Spirit has begun to make in the converts' lives, and leads them to a greater awareness of personal responsibility for their attitudes and actions. Celebration services are geared to promote and support this process, using the Christian calendar to ensure that all the main seasons are reflected in the worship – Advent, Lent, Good Friday, Easter Saturday Vigil, Easter Sunday, Pentecost, etc. Worship is further enriched with Scripture readings, preaching and teaching throughout the year. Generally the team leader decides on a particular set of readings as a focus for the preaching in a given season, and the celebration leaders give whatever emphasis is appropriate to the specific pastoral needs of the people for whom they have oversight at other times. In this way, themes are followed rather than the particularities of the lectionary. All who preach at St Thomas's are encouraged to be the voice (*vox*) of the word (*verbum*), and hence to preach biblically for a clear response (Isaiah 55:11).

Most teaching in St Thomas's is carried out at the level of small groups and clusters. Short study courses on such diverse subjects as Old and New Testament studies, systematic theology, church history and many other topics relating to Christian life, mission and ministry are offered at various times throughout the year, as well as the seminars which are part of the normal conference and Second Sunday programmes. During Advent, Lent and Holy Week, evening meditation services are held which usually include a short address or teaching section.

For the emerging generation, the importance of belonging and the life-changing effect of the kingdom of God have led to a hunger for something more substantial than the normal life of the church in terms of learning to face the call of God on their lives. In 1995 a programme called the Young Adult

Placement Scheme (YAPS), now called Tribal Training, was inaugurated to meet this demand. Seven candidates applied for the first year and were accepted on the basis that they would serve the church for 21 hours a week for one year, at their own expense, supplementing their financial needs through part-time employment. Initially they were assigned to a staff member, accompanying them on their round of duties. Set periods for Bible study and theological reflection through formal teaching and involvement with different departments of the church's life became tools for laying foundations and values to be used in their future life. The scheme has gone from strength to strength. For the academic year beginning in 2001, 34 applicants were accepted. This has spawned identical schemes in other churches: 25 candidates at a church in Cheltenham, 15 in London and 28 in Dublin. Some older members expressed a desire for similar input into their lives, and so the Mature Adult Placement Scheme (MAPS) was also started. One hundred and ten people have completed the course so far, several of whom are now involved as full- or part-time members of staff, or leaders of clusters within the church.

Following the methodology of the early church, St Thomas's seeks to make the gospel relevant without diluting its message, and this has meant adapting to the varying needs of the Builders, Boomers and Busters. Commenting on the surrounding culture in the days of the early church, Ray C. Stedman observes, 'The gospel germinated in a social climate – a time of injustice, racial division, social unrest, rampant crime, unbridled immorality, economic uncertainty, and widespread fear.'[1] St Thomas's recognises such a situation as not dissimilar to the state of the world

---

[1] Ray C. Stedman, *Bodylife* (Discovery House Publishers, 1972), p. 35.

today, and is working hard to follow God's guidance in meeting the needs of its community with the gospel.

Potential conflict with the institutional church

St Thomas's does church in a way which appears to many to be unorthodox. Critics of our methodology would accuse us of deconstructing the institution of the church. Membership requirements, ecumenism, low emphasis on denominational affiliation, and charismatic spirituality do not resonate with the practice of most traditional denominational churches. Some consider the charismatic approach to be manipulative, opening the gates of fear and surrender in those who are emotionally vulnerable. However, if the process of proclaiming the message of the gospel enables people to be transformed, renewed, healed and restored, it is hard to classify that as a negative dimension in the church's proclamation.

The modern process in Christianity of using the format of 'behaving, believing and belonging' to spread the faith has seen some degree of success. Nonetheless, living as we now do in a post-Christian, post-denominational and postmodern world, we believe that the order of this approach needs to be changed, so that 'belonging' comes first, then 'believing', which leads on to 'behaving'.

Not wishing to be in direct conflict with the denominational structures represented at St Thomas's, we have a sincere desire to effect change from within whenever possible. This includes electing suitable people to represent St Thomas's at various committee levels in both streams, to ensure meaningful dialogue with those in authority and to keep them informed of policy developments at St Thomas's itself.

Recent discussions have involved revisiting and re-evaluating models which have served the church effectively in similar situations in the past. In particular, as explained below, the potential of the 'minster model' seems to favour the current context of pluralism and rapid change in the church in the UK. One of the advantages is that it appears to be an acceptable format of church practice for Anglicans, and it also resonates with institutional ecclesiastical language, albeit from the distant past.

Using Celtic monastery and minster models for mission

Sheffield is rapidly developing in its economic and commercial life, as a centre for education, and in its significance as a city in the northern region of England. St Thomas's likewise began to grow in reputation and influence, developing its ministry in both the city centre and the parish church at Crookes. As a consequence, teams from St Thomas's were regularly requested to carry out missions in other churches, cities and nations, and these in turn proved to be so successful that many church leaders began to make pilgrimage to St Thomas's from all parts of the world. Like the Wise Men of old, their expressed aim was to see for themselves the thing that God was doing in our midst, of which they had heard news and seen signs. They wanted to worship him here, and then return to their homelands to report what they had experienced so that they could discern how they might use St Thomas's methods and principles of mission to their advantage in their own situations. We continue to receive a steady stream of such visitors and constant requests to share our resources and staff time. Thanks to this, the values of St Thomas's missiological framework have found their way to many different parts of the globe.

In the last few years, it has been recognised that St Thomas's is indeed growing into the kind of 'Ephesus resource church' that the Lord had seemed to suggest it would. In 1997, a member of the Anglican Church Planting Initiatives staff, Revd Bob Hopkins (also now a member of St Thomas's staff), made a presentation to a national meeting of archdeacons at Church House, Westminster. This was a special focus meeting convened by the Board of Mission of the General Synod to look at the areas of parish ministry, network relationships and mission strategy. Bob Hopkins proposed that the example of St Thomas's, with its growing network of churches, had the potential to lead to a significant 'urban movement for mission' and the planting of many missiological communities. The idea was taken to a further national archdeacons' meeting the following year.

Additionally, in sections 2.49–2.51 of the Strategy Report of Sheffield Diocese (1999–2004), St Thomas's was further described as a 'minster church'. This was helpful in that it placed the work and influence of St Thomas's within a recognisable ecclesiastical framework. Historically, an English minster was staffed by clerics and monks under orders and included both single and married lay members. The staff community, or *familia*, typically included an inner circle of senior priests and minor clerks, whose life was undergirded by prayer and worship. The more important minsters also had schools attached, where young adults would be trained for leadership and prepared for holy orders.[2] These were considered to be

---

[2] See John Godfrey, 'The English Parish: 600–1300', *Church History Outlines* No. 3 (SPCK, 1969).

centres of academic excellence, and the 'graduates' were sought after for many different roles within society.[3]

For St Thomas's, however, the minster model is only part of the picture. The Celtic monastic movement provides another important element. Although it is difficult to generalise, it seems that Celtic monasteries regularly sent out mobile mission teams to proclaim the gospel to the pre-Christian tribes of Europe. These Celtic missionaries (known as *peregrini* or *gyrovagi*) would simply 'go for the love of Christ'. Some teams were led by a bishop with the expressed intention of planting Christian communities among the unreached people groups of the day.

When members were sent out from the parish church at Crookes, its numbers grew. The city-centre venue became an environment where small groups and clusters who had a heart to reach out to the city could think beyond the normal geographical limits of the parish. The missionary vision which was nurtured in these early clusters led to them being known affectionately as 'eagles' nests' (Deuteronomy 32:11). This was to prove prophetic, for all too soon – as in the biblical analogy – these nests were stirred.

When our city-centre venue was suddenly no longer available to us, the clusters took to the wing – and found they could fly! They settled wherever they could find safe lodging, some in homes, others in cinemas, cafés, garages, even other churches. Such forced dispersion into different regions of the city and, more especially, into a kaleidoscope of venues (truly represen-

---

[3] The universities of Durham, Cambridge and Oxford, for example, developed out of such minster 'academies', with the faculty of theology often being the first established.

tative of the subcultures of the postmodern world), served to multiply St Thomas's further, adding to our number those who were being saved. This follows the repeated biblical pattern of concentration and spread, as described in the book of Acts. As in the early church, where hard circumstances forced the apostles and pioneers outwards (Acts 8:1b), so our circumstances forced us into doing church in alternative ways. This pattern continues to the present day. Some of those pioneering missional groups are now looking to multiply again, because growth has meant that they need to set out once more and find bigger venues than those in which they initially settled.

A postmodern synthesis

At St Thomas's we believe that we need to take the scriptural references to Ephesus and the historical principles and practices of both the Celtic monastic movement and the ancient minster churches, and weave them together into a synthesis. This is how we believe we can define the charism – or call – of St Thomas's as it seeks under God to develop a pragmatic movement for mission, relevant to the twenty-first century. We sense that using such a synthesis would make us effective in reaching the emerging generation with its fast-moving, highly mobile postmodern culture.

This charism began to find external and institutional confirmation in the discussions that took place in 2000 between Mike Breen, the Archbishop of York and the Bishop of Sheffield. As a result, the official formation and launch of an Order of Mission from St Thomas's Church is now a distinct possibility. In June 2002 a draft proposal for the Rule and Constitution of the Order of Mission of St Thomas's Church was formally offered to the Advisory Council on Religious Communities of the Anglican Church, and it was received with much enthusiasm. Similar discussions are taking place with the denominational officers of the Baptist Union of Great Britain and the Yorkshire Baptist Association.

Our aim is to plant two saplings – one symbolising the traditional institutional denominations and the other representing a unique new missionary order. Our hope and prayer is that in this way a new phase of history might be entered into in the life of the whole church, progressing the apostolic mission of God in the postmodern world. As time passes, we would hope that these saplings continue to grow and work together in a spirit of unity and faith, building on the foundation that has already been laid at the parish church, but also following the example of those who have gone before – monks and missionaries, religious orders, circuit preachers, bishops and priests alike.

The ratification of such a movement as the Order of Mission of St Thomas's Church could strengthen the existing resolve to work together in accountable relationship in order to spread scriptural holiness throughout the land and fulfil Christ's Great Commission (Matthew 28:18–20). New avenues for the mutual sharing of experiences and resources within the wider church could be opened up, encouraging all members to employ kingdom values and relevant missiological methods in the work of reaching the emerging generation for Christ.

The charism of the Order of Mission of St Thomas's Church – vision, gift, task and call

The Order of Mission of St Thomas's Church seeks to participate in the general *missio Dei* alongside other ministries of the universal church, yet at the same time be obedient to the specific expression of this mission which it understands as its distinctive charism.

While recognising the validity and importance of the ministry, gifting and calling of all Christians, the Order of Mission of St Thomas's Church intentionally seeks to identify, train, disciple and release missional leaders – 'pioneering pilgrims' who have avowed their lives first of all to God. Training would include specific teaching and the development of ministry and leadership gifting, alongside personal discipleship within the context of a mentoring relationship and 'huddle' (a group of up to 12 being discipled together). Missional leaders would be formally commissioned and sent out as members of the Order, but always expected to operate in community and as teams. Some might be locally ordained, operating within the context of the Order. A reputable academic 'visitor of ordinands' would be responsible for overseeing their theological preparation for ministry and mission, as required by the denominations involved.

Provision would also be made for other clergy to transfer and serve as missional leaders within the Order, rather than as pastors and priests within the traditional structures of their respective denominations. The intended task for all missional leaders would be to initiate and inspire new expressions of church and to establish and resource 'mission order communities' and churches. They would be expected to seek to understand and engage with the culture in which they live and serve, and in particular reach out to the emerging generation. They would operate under the authority of a relevant senior and at the direction of the superior. A 'visitor of missionaries' would advise and oversee their development for this missiological task.

In time some missional leaders would take up long-term assignments (*stabilitas*) in order to ensure that the DNA – the vision and values – of the Order are caught by osmosis as well as taught. Discussions have already taken place with overseas network leaders, and we would expect some appointments to be undertaken in those countries, as well as in other cities and regions of the UK and Ireland.

Other missional leaders would engage in shorter-term mission trips, both at home and abroad, focusing more on resourcing the wider church through existing parishes and churches seeking to use the vocabulary of values and theology in their setting. Yet others would be based at the mother church (initially at St Thomas's), thus ensuring that the life, charism and spiritual dynamic are maintained at the centre as well as being sent out 'to the edge'. All leaders would be required to live out a commitment to the Rule of the Order of Mission of St Thomas's Church, and would be specifically encouraged to grow to greater maturity in the spiritual disciplines of prayer, work, study and fasting.[4]

Since monasticism has existed since the second century, many of the founders of new religious orders in the past were educated, experienced and passionate men and women of faith who actually began by entering the ranks of an existing institution. When they took an honest look at the world and church of their day, they found a sad and sorry situation and much that had no permanent value. In order to revive mission work, they set out to produce a new set of values – expressed in a Rule of

---

[4] Devoted to a life of simplicity, purity and accountability and living a common life (IN), sustained by a discipline of common worship and prayer (UP), and issuing in works that are primarily of a public nature (OUT).

Life. A Rule was never intended to displace the gospel (the supreme rule) in any way, but rather to act as a better way of applying the gospel practically to the circumstances of daily life, not only at the individual level but also in the new communities of faith they planned to create. In time, what developed was a form of enhanced living, growth and a disciplined community faithful to Scripture. The principles of their Rule committed them to mission in their own cultural milieu, as well as to meeting the needs of the wider church, which was often failing in its role.

Religious orders are still recognised as forces for pioneering mission, renewal and evangelism within the church, and indeed often act as a prophetic voice to the world. The current state of the church in the West seems to suggest that there is a need for more of them, working to provide a new rule appropriate to the spiritual and cultural climate, and helping people to live out the gospel and share its good news with the current generation. Statistics demonstrate how badly the institutional forms of church (in all denominations) are haemorrhaging in terms of committed membership, failing to attract new converts to the faith community in spite of specific drives such as the Decade of Evangelism.

St Thomas's has shown that the task of pioneering leadership and mission can be greatly enhanced through the active and ongoing deployment of all five ministries of the church as described in Ephesians 4. The Lifeskills course has proved invaluable and inspirational in this respect. Under the Rule of St Thomas's, provision would be made for periodic retreat and renewal at the mother church for all seniors, guardians (who will be the overseers of apostles, prophets, evangelists, pastors and teachers), missional leaders and members. By such means the identity and purpose of the Order would be maintained, using the potential of postmodernism with its bias towards the active dimension of mission, constantly fuelled and supported by drawing on the contemplative tradition of the ancient church.

St Thomas's has already experienced the advantages of being enriched in this way, from the fusion of the Anglican and Baptist traditions at the formation of the LEP, which freed the church to operate in a different way and laid the foundations for its current mission. In many respects, therefore, the church has already demonstrated that such an apparently abnormal method of operating can meet with a fair degree of success. The church's history thus suggests that establishing a mission order is a route worth pursuing.

The challenge for twenty-first-century mission

Doing church in a way which 'democratises the sacred' and is relevant to the prevailing cultural milieu, which reinforces the sense of belonging, will invariably make mission to the emerging generation more accessible. Of necessity, this implies many structural adaptations, but at St Thomas's we believe that the challenge posed by contemporary culture should be viewed as a window of opportunity rather than as a difficulty to be overcome. The church members of the first century had to present the same message to their culture with its own attendant set of challenges. They did it in a way which was actively lived out at an individual as well as a community level, making the necessary adjustments to the culture without any dilution of the message. Paul's commendation to the Colossian church is an insight into the success of such a witness: 'All over the world this gospel is bearing fruit and growing' (Colossians 1:6).

St Thomas's has decided it is worth the effort to move in this direction, and it has continued to embrace whatever changes are necessary to fulfil the call to reach the emerging generation for Christ. Ian Pitt-Watson encapsulates the enormous possibilities when he discusses the power of the message which a preacher carries into the pulpit each week, and which is often underestimated by those authorised to preach: 'There is nothing in all creation, nothing in human experience of joy or pain, nothing in all the physical world from the galaxies to the atom that cannot be a theophany, a Christophany, a revelation of God in Christ.'[5]

The peculiarities of our place, time and circumstances are not a hindrance to the message of the gospel. The seedbed already exists, and there has never been a greater time than the present to further the kingdom. Since the birth of the church, the Holy Spirit has empowered believers to such an extent that they turned the world upside down. Philip and the refugees from Jerusalem, on the way to Samaria, 'preached the word wherever they went' (Acts 8:4). Paul and Barnabas, sent out by the church in Antioch (Acts 13), did the same, as did their successors. The message was the same, but the methodology was always subservient to the truth it contained. Charles Spurgeon, in the nineteenth century, recognised this fact:

> Believing, therefore, that there is such a thing as truth, and such a thing as falsehood, that there are truths in the Bible, and the Gospel consists of something definite which is believed by men, it becomes

---

[5] Ian Pitt-Watson, *A Primer for Preachers* (Baker, 1986), p. 28.

us to be decided as to what to teach, and to teach in a decided manner. We have to deal with men who will either be lost or saved, and they will not be saved by erroneous doctrine.[6]

Such is the challenge, and such are the possibilities, of meeting the spiritual hunger of the emerging generation with the true food of the gospel. However we may tackle this challenge, we must remain biblically based. Otherwise the church becomes just one of the many and varied ways to a form of truth, and not the distinctive and unique path to Jesus as Lord.

[6] John W. Doberstein, *The Minister's Prayer Book* (Collins, 1986), p. 24.

Conclusion

When Jesus left this earth to go to heaven he left no one else to do the work of the kingdom except those who make up the church. There is no 'Plan B', nor are there resources tantamount to the 'arrival of the cavalry' to help the church in its current difficulties, other than those who make up its members at a local level. The tools available to them are those described in 1 Corinthians 12 and the way to use them is outlined in Romans 12, using the 'grace given as Christ apportioned' – the grace given to each member to operate as an apostle, prophet, evangelist, pastor or teacher, as described in Ephesians 4. St Thomas's Lifeskills course provides an accessible and easily transferable means of working out these principles.

Since it is clear that no further outside resources are available, the conclusion must be that this represents the order of things in the church, and not church order. In this respect, coming to terms with the objective fact that God's anointing is upon a believer (UP), having it affirmed by those within the church

(IN), and then working it through (OUT), requires a greater degree of personal responsibility than is the norm.

At face value this may appear to be an endorsement of the individualism prevalent in current culture. This is not so. Such a paradigm shift, however, can be traumatic for both members and leaders. For most members, 'church' is doing what the clergy or leaders say, and if it is not successful then those in charge can be blamed. This also avoids the embarrassment of following the instruction to 'submit to one another out of reverence for Christ' (Ephesians 5:21) – something which, unfortunately, we find hard to do thanks to our privatised, individualistic society. Nonetheless, if the IN dimension is applied as described in the 'learning circle' in Chapter 7 (see page 134), accountability and responsibility for actions stops people from having a 'roller coaster' faith where high points of closeness to God are superseded by events around them or failure to live a life of holiness. This is because the body acting as a community of faith precludes individualism. In addition, leaders are able to exercise oversight, direction and counsel to enable members to use all the gifts God has provided.

We accept that not everyone will agree with our interpretation of how to do church, but at St Thomas's we have discovered that our approach allows members to work out their faith creatively, operating together as a body and within a clear framework for living. Not only has this facilitated growth, it has also created a community of believers who feel they 'belong' to one another as the family of God. In this regard we feel we have a vital message to offer to the wider church.

We have no intention of decrying the significant contribution made by the institutional church, but even that body admits to facing a life-threatening crisis. Part of the problem is a lack of belief that God still reaches out to his people, and this form of theological agnosticism has affected those in leadership positions. Where is the anticipation of God's real presence? Where is the expectation of the Spirit's activity? At St Thomas's we are not deliberately setting out to be radical or even schismatic. Our sincere desire is to see a reversal of fortunes for the church at large, to see the kingdom extended and vigorous, healthy growth taking place. Such a move involves going back to first principles, which are still reflected – though arguably unappreciated – in the liturgy of most traditional churches. The most important of these principles is to believe that when the Lord of the church and his Holy Spirit are asked to come, they come with all majesty, glory and power.

We would also make a plea for consistency of Christian witness and service. Cultural, philosophical and theological perspectives which are accessible to the whole church can and must be developed, in order to contribute to a greater understanding of what it means to be the discerning people of God in his kingdom. The idea that God is there and is not silent, and is on the record as continuing the plan which was there 'before the creation of the world' (1 Peter 1:20), should hold no problems for the church. This 'realised' aspect needs to be affirmed and practised, however, if it is to have any significance for the credibility and integrity of God. If it does not, then those of us who have put our trust in him are false witnesses, and grace, the unmerited free love of God, becomes an empty shell.

The church in every age and every place has had to come to terms with its cultural setting and with the worldview of the people it seeks to win under the calling of the Great Commission. I hope the overview in Chapter 3 of the characteristics of the generations that make up our current cultural setting has offered some insight into the peculiarities of modern mission in the UK and the West. With such a dearth of effective evangelism and mission in our land, we face the greatest mission challenge in the world. It is somewhat ironic, when I visit Nigeria, to be asked by Christians there, 'Why does the church in the UK not do what the missionaries told us to do?' Why, that is, do we not preach the gospel and act as missionaries in an arena where there is such an obvious need? The prospects of a Mission Order as described in Chapter 9 will, we hope, provide the impetus and resources to help the church move forward in just such a mission.

In Chapter 2 I detailed the personal spiritual journey which led me to St Thomas's. At times this has involved determined acts of will in order to transcend my scepticism that such expectations could be tolerated, never mind put into practice. So far it has been worth it. Had I listened to those who doubted whether an LEP with Anglicans could work, or had I accepted the cessationists' position that the gifts of the Holy Spirit were not for today, or had I listened to the criticism of other church leaders who regard St Thomas's approach as going against the interests of the institutional church, I would have been deprived of a most exhilarating experience. As it is, I have seen dynamic and inspirational proof of the effect of the kingdom of God at work in a local church situation. I empathise with St Joan, as depicted by George Bernard Shaw, when she was confronted by the Archbishop of Rheims and members of the French court who asserted that her voices were not from God. She told them:

I see now that the loneliness of God is his strength. What would he be if he listened to all your jealous little councils? Well, my loneliness shall be my strength too: it is better to be alone with God. His friendship will not fail me, nor his counsel, nor his love. In his strength I will dare and dare and dare until I die.[1]

The most important lesson I have learned from being part of the leadership at St Thomas's is that Christ is Lord of the church. It is he who will build it, and he gives himself unreservedly to that end. He has no plan to win the world other than through the empowering of his Spirit. As Paul puts it, 'he made known to us the mystery of his will' (Ephesians 1:9). The depths of God's unsearchable riches are there to be plumbed, and all our senses should be employed to ensure that we do his will. All that we need has been provided – and at St Thomas's, using the methodology described in this book, we have seen many added to the kingdom, for which we praise God.

---

[1] George Bernard Shaw, *Saint Joan* (Penguin Books, 1951), p. 112.

St Thomas's Ministry Questionnaire

Instructions for users

1. Pray that God will take this time and use it to reveal his will for individuals; that blessing would flow from him to the participants and in turn to other people.
2. Read Ephesians 4:1–13 and discuss the character of the five ministries briefly. Express the value of knowing which you identify with most.
3. Meditate and pray at length to ask God to reveal your ministries.
4. The questionnaire itself takes about 10 minutes to complete and the scoring may take a further 10–15 minutes. The general emphasis is for subtlety rather than the blindingly obvious, to avoid as much as possible people's humility or arrogance, so that they cannot easily stick with what they think they are. Questions are designed to cover different aspects of each ministry 'character' rather than always giving the obvious 'typical' definition. Ultimately the questionnaire

may work better for suggesting what you are *not*, so that you can focus on the other possibilities. More mature and experienced Christians who have theoretically been through more 'phases' are likely to tick 'sometimes' more often, which will balance out the scores and therefore prove indecisive – except to say that they are well rounded! 'Often', 'Sometimes' and 'Rarely' should be considered in a general sense, not in the context of your personal experiences – i.e. how often you do something compared to other people, rather than what proportion of your time you spend on that activity. The idea is to compare yourself with the behaviour of everyone else, to determine how you differ.

5. Share the results within your small group. Often other people are better at recognising our giftings than we are ourselves.

6. Pray together for God to confirm, or otherwise, the results. A flawed questionnaire is no substitute for seeking God's calling on your life through prayer and experience.

What are they?

Apostle: A pioneering ministry made up of those who are sent. It may be difficult to decide for yourself that you are an apostle, but if you generally identify yourself with 'apostolic' type activities, you may well fit into this category. Not to be mistaken for 'Apostle' in the sense of someone of high hierarchical authority in the church with a powerful leadership position (or someone with a specific throne reserved for them in heaven!).

Prophet: A ministry of listening to God and sharing what you hear.

Evangelist: A ministry of telling the good news of the kingdom. Involved in helping the church to grow from the outside, but also in encouraging the witness and testimony of others.

Pastor: A ministry of caring for the people for whom God has given you responsibility.

Teacher: A ministry of instructing people in the truth about God. Not necessarily someone who knows a lot, or who likes to tell other people what they know. A more appropriate test is whether or not people understand, remember and implement the things you say, i.e. 'learn'.

Item no.		Often	Some-times	Rarely
1	I remember names or at least where I first met someone			
2	I have expressed my feelings about God as pictures or analogies			
3	My ability to present Scripture clearly and accurately has been commented on			
4	I can be counted on to contribute original ideas			
5	I find myself talking about my faith to the people I meet			
6	I get frustrated when I feel I'm not experiencing 'new' things as a Christian			
7	When I communicate biblical truths to others I see resulting changes in knowledge, attitudes, values or conduct			
8	I share what knowledge I have with others			
9	I have an urge to share thoughts with people that I felt when I prayed and I have been told they meant something or were relevant to the person's current situation			
10	I get upset at other people's difficulties and problems even if I haven't experienced them myself			

11	I have a strong sense of what God wants to say to people in response to a particular situation					
12	I enjoy studying the Scriptures and find that I get fresh insights that people find interesting and helpful					
13	When reading the Bible I am more able to grasp the wider picture or message than the specific details					
14	I like to share what I believe					
15	I have been successful in developing Christian discipline in others					
16	I'll try things out if it will encourage others to do the same					
17	I am quick to help when help is needed and often do things which I see need to be done without even being asked					
18	I have been able to spot a 'person of peace' who is ready to receive a word from God and have seen a positive response					
19	I have a clear vision and others have said that they feel confident to go along with me					
20	I try explaining things in different ways if people are finding a concept difficult to grasp or understand					
21	I think before I speak					

Item no.		Often	Some-times	Rarely
22	I really fear that people I know will not be saved			
23	I like to be clear and decisive when speaking about what I believe God has said to me			
24	I am by no means an expert on Scripture, but I can grasp the point of a passage quite quickly			
25	I get frustrated and even depressed at the lack of faith or understanding of others around me			
26	People tell me that the things I say often help them to try new things for God			
27	I am interested in living and working overseas or among people from a different culture			
28	I am good at listening and taking in what people say			
29	I have contrived situations so that non-Christians are prompted to ask spiritual questions			
30	I have helped fellow believers by guiding them to relevant portions of the Bible			
31	I get excited when I discover new understanding, insights and applications of God's word			

32	I have reminded people of the foundations of their faith						
33	Despite not enjoying the nitty-gritty details of leadership, I still often end up leading things						
34	People have told me that I have helped them be restored to the Christian community						
35	I feel that I know exactly what God wants to do in ministry at a specific point in time						
36	I dig out information and passages to explain a concept						
37	I mix easily with a wide variety of people without having to try to be one of them						
38	I have a deep concern to encourage people towards spiritual growth and achievement						
39	I try to think of different ways of expressing the truth of the gospel						
40	Friends ask me to help clarify a situation or scripture						
41	I am quite persuasive when encouraging people to examine their spiritual motives						
42	I empathise with those who are hurting or broken and can support them through their pain to wholeness						

Item no.		Often	Some-times	Rarely
43	When in a group, I am the one others often look to for vision and direction			
44	I enjoy being with non-believers because of my desire to win them to Christ			
45	I will see a job through to the end so that no one has to pick up the pieces after me			
46	My prayers surprise me with their clarity and unexpected direction			
47	People comment that they remember what I tell them about God			
48	I *expect* opportunities for witnessing to arise rather than react in surprise when they occur			
49	I desire the gift of healing in greater measure (that the Lord would heal others through me)			
50	The things I say in a spiritual context make people feel uncomfortable			
51	I have enjoyed relating to a certain group of people over a period of time, sharing personally in their successes and their failures			
52	People have told me that I have helped them learn biblical truth in a meaningful way			
53	I have led someone to a decision for salvation through faith in Christ			

54	God has enabled me to reveal specific things which have happened or meant something at a later date			
55	There have been times when I felt sure I knew God's specific will for the future growth of his work, even when others have not been so sure			
56	People have told me that I have communicated timely words or pictures which must have come directly from the Lord			
57	People call on me to help those who are less fortunate			
58	I get great satisfaction from studying the Bible and sharing my insights with others			
59	Others have suggested that I am a person of unusual vision			
60	Non-Christians have noted that they feel comfortable when they are around me, and that I have a positive effect on them towards developing a faith in Christ			
61	I am willing to challenge or confront people in order to help them mature			
62	I regularly need to get space alone or long periods of time out to reflect, pray and think			
63	I have just suddenly known something about someone			
64	I enjoy taking notes when someone is speaking and pay close attention to the details of what they are saying			

Item no.		Often	Some-times	Rarely
65	I am faithful in providing support, care and nurture for others over long periods of time, even when others have stopped			
66	I enjoy mentoring individuals			
67	I enjoy relating stories and sharing my experiences			
68	I enjoy coming up with new and original ideas, dreaming big and thinking about visions for the future			
69	I find non-Christians ask me questions about my faith in Christ, and my church involvement			
70	I can accurately assess a person based on first impressions and know instinctively when something is not quite right			
71	I like to provide a safe and comfortable environment where people feel they are welcome, that they belong, are listened to and cared for			
72	I would like to start a church or a new ministry in an area which is not catered for at present			
73	I have a heart to share my faith and to pray for those in my work and neighbourhood who do not attend church			
74	When I hear about situations of need I feel burdened to pray			

75	I like to help churches, organisations, groups and leaders become more efficient and often find myself thinking about how things function			
76	I enjoy spending time studying Scripture and prefer to do so systematically			
77	I look for opportunities to socialise and to build relationships with non-Christians			
78	People come to me to ask me my opinion on particular parts of the Bible or to answer their queries			
79	I find that people trust me and come to me regularly, wanting to chat and looking for my advice, prayers and help			
80	I can clarify goals, develop strategies, and use resources effectively to accomplish tasks			

Now transfer your answers to the score sheet on the facing page and add up your totals.

- Place a tick against each item number for which you answered 'often' or 'sometimes' (the 'rarely' answers are not counted, but you may wish to use the shaded column for 'rarely' to keep tabs on which answers you have transferred from the question sheet).
- Note that some numbers occur more than once in the columns on the score sheet.
- Finally, add up the number of 'often' ticks, double the answer and add to the number of ticks for 'sometimes'. Refer to the 'Results' boxes on p. 214.

Remember this is only a snapshot. If you want to use the questionnaire to provide a more accurate picture, you will have to use it on several occasions in the future and keep your results to compare. I think that if you used the questionnaire two or three times a year for two or three years you would begin to get a clear picture both of your base ministry and of the phases you were most regularly visiting.

Block 1

Item no.	A Often	B Some-times	C Rarely
1			
10			
17			
21			
28			
30			
34			
42			
45			
49			
51			
57			
53			
60			
65			
66			
71			
79			

Totals: A [ ] B [ ] C [ ] D [ ]

Multiply total in A by 2 = [ ]

Grand total (B + D) = [ ]

Block 2

Item no.	A Often	B Some-times	C Rarely
2			
9			
11			
23			
25			
31			
35			
41			
46			
50			
54			
56			
27			
55			
62			
63			
70			
74			

Totals: A [ ] B [ ] C [ ] D [ ]

Multiply total in A by 2 = [ ]

Grand total (B + D) = [ ]

Block 3

Item no.	A Often	B Some-times	C Rarely
3			
7			
8			
12			
15			
20			
24			
36			
40			
47			
52			
58			
21			
39			
64			
67			
76			
78			

Totals: A [ ] B [ ] C [ ] D [ ]

Multiply total in A by 2 = [ ]

Grand total (B + D) = [ ]

Block 4

Item no.	A Often	B Some-times	C Rarely
5			
14			
18			
22			
29			
32			
37			
39			
44			
48			
53			
60			
1			
51			
61			
69			
73			
77			

Totals: A [ ] B [ ] C [ ] D [ ]

Multiply total in A by 2 = [ ]

Grand total (B + D) = [ ]

Block 5

Item no.	A Often	B Some-times	C Rarely
4			
6			
13			
16			
19			
26			
27			
33			
38			
43			
55			
59			
32			
11			
68			
72			
75			
80			

Totals: A [ ] B [ ] C [ ] D [ ]

Multiply total in A by 2 = [ ]

Grand total (B + D) = [ ]

Results of questionnaire

Working from left to right, transfer the grand totals shown on page 213 to the boxes below to discover your base and phase ministries.

Grand total   Grand total   Grand total   Grand total   Grand total

☐   ☐   ☐   ☐   ☐

PASTOR   PROPHET   TEACHER   EVANGELIST   APOSTLE

The Order of Mission

The Order of Mission (TOM) was formally launched on Sunday 6th April 2003 in Sheffield by the Archbishop of York as a religious community to identify, train, disciple and release Missional Leaders who have committed their lives under God to the initiation and development of new expressions of church.

In its early stages the structure, shape and texture of TOM will be evolutionary and provisional. As its size and influence increases a constitution will be developed to give appropriate form and structure to the work of the Order.

All religious orders use a rule based on scriptural principles by which the lives of their members are ordered, and which describes the *spiritual DNA* of the movement. The traditional monastic concepts of poverty, chastity and obedience are reinterpreted in the rule of TOM as devotion to a life of simplicity, purity and accountability as well as the Lifeskills principles of UP, IN and OUT (see Chapter 7).

Three levels are open to those in leadership positions in the church:

- **Temporary membership:** Broadly paralleling the Novitiate in traditional monastic orders, a three-year period as a Temporary member of TOM provides time necessary for a person to test their calling to permanent membership of TOM.

- **Permanent membership:** If, after three years, it is agreed that a Temporary is called to life within the Order, they will be invited to take permanent vows. Under normal circumstances these are binding for life. For this reason, a married person cannot be a Permanent unless their spouse is, at least, an Associate.

- **Associate membership:** Those who wish to be involved in the work of TOM, whether through prayer, finance, or in other ways, and who do not wish to undertake temporary membership, may become Associates. This may be particularly appropriate to those who feel that the demands of life within the Order would be incompatible with other demands on them at the time, such as, for example, the needs of their family, or a prior commitment to another contemporary move of God.

It is not intended that churches should become Order churches, though a church leader may be a member and their church may be affiliated to the Order through them.

The work of the Order will include:

- Tasks necessary for the administration, ordering and functioning of the Order.
- Ministries for which the Order accepts a special responsibility – apostolic, prophetic, evangelistic, pastoral and teaching roles.

- Work in the wider church for the sake of its unity, mission, spiritual life, support, resourcing and education.
- Work in society, not least for the sake of the poor and disadvantaged, the oppressed and victims of injustice.
- Pioneering new expressions of church and establishing Missional Communities and reaching out to the emerging generation.

Oversight of the work of TOM and its members will be the particular responsibility of the Superior and his representatives. Members are not free to undertake commitments on their own authority, but should be ready to make suggestions for the development of their own work and that of the Order.

TOM recognises the importance of life-long learning, which may include training for specific tasks. Members are encouraged to identify areas for further personal study and training.

For further details contact:

Dean of Admissions
St Thomas Church
Philadelphia Campus
Gilpin Street
Sheffield S3 6BL

www.stthomaschurch.org.uk

Bibliography

Abbot, T.K., *The International Critical Commentary: The Epistles to the Ephesians and to the Colossians,* T & T Clark, 1909

The Alternative Service Book, SPCK, 1980

Anderson, Ray S., *The Soul of Ministry*, Westminster John Knox Press, 1997

Anker, Roy, *Dancing in the Dark*, Bridgepoint, 1991

The Baptist Union Directory for 1991–92, Gem Publishing Company, 1992

Banks, Robert, *Paul's Idea of Community*, Eerdmans, 1980

Barna, George, *The Second Coming of the Church*, Word, 1998

Barrett, C.K., *The Signs of an Apostle*, Paternoster Press, 1996

Barth, Karl, *The Epistle to the Romans*, trans. Edwyn C. Hoskyns, Oxford University Press, 1968

Barth, Markus, *Ephesians 4–6*, Doubleday & Co., 1960

Berkouwer, G.C., *General Revelation*, Eerdmans, 1955

Blanchard, Kenneth, Zigarmi and Drea Zigarmi, *The One-Minute Manager*, HarperCollins Publishers, 1986

Bloch-Hoell, Nihls, *The Pentecostal Movement*, Allen & Unwin, 1964

The Book of Common Prayer, Eyre & Spottiswoode Limited

Bornkamm, Günther, *Early Christian Experience*, SCM Press, 1966

Brayfield, Celia, 'Generation Bland', *The Times*, 7 August 2000, Section 2, p. 3

Breen, Mike, *Growing the Smaller Church*, Marshall Pickering, 1992

——, *Outside In*, Scripture Union, 1993

——, *The Body Beautiful*, Monarch, 1997

Brierley, Peter, *The Tide Is Running Out*, Christian Research, 2000

Brown, Colin (ed.), *The Dictionary of New Testament Theology, Vol. 2*, Paternoster Press, 1976

Bruce, F.F., *Men and Movements in the Primitive Church*, Paternoster Press, 1979

Buckingham, Marcus and Curt Coffman, *First Break All the Rules*, Simon & Schuster, 1999

Bugbee, Bruce, *What You Do Best in the Body of Christ*, Zondervan Publishing House, 1995

Calvin, John, *Institutes of the Christian Religion*, ed. John T. McNeill, trans. Ford Lewis Battles, The Westminster Press, 1960

Carson, D.A., *Showing the Spirit*, Paternoster Press, 1995

Cartledge, Mark J., 'Charismatic Prophecy: A Definition and Description', *Journal of Pentecostal Theology*, 5 (1994), pp. 79–120

Clark, Andrew C., 'Apostleship: Evidence from the New Testament and Early Christian Literature', *Vox Evangelica XIX* (1989), pp. 49–82

Conger, Yves, *The Word and the Spirit*, Harper Row Publishers, 1984

Dawn, Marva J., *Reaching Out Without Dumbing Down*, Eerdmans, 1995

Doberstein, John W., *The Minister's Prayer Book*, Collins, 1986

Dowley, Tim, *A Lion Handbook: The History of Christianity*, Lion Publishing, 1977

Driver, John, *Images of the Church in Mission*, Herald Press, 1997

Dunn, James, *Unity and Diversity in the New Testament*, SCM, 1977

——, *Word Biblical Commentary, Vol. 38, Romans 9–16*, Word Publishers, 1988

Ekman, Ulf, *The Apostolic Ministry*, Kingsway, 1993

Fee, Gordon D., *God's Empowering Presence*, Hendrickson Publishers, 1994

Finney, John, *Church on the Move*, Darton, Longman & Todd, 1992

——, *Recovering the Past*, Darton, Longman & Todd, 1996

Fiske, John, *Understanding Popular Culture*, Rootledge Chapman Hall, 1989

Foulkes, Francis, *Ephesians*, Eerdmans, 1983

Gallup, Jr., George and D. Michael Lindsay, *Surveying the Religious Landscape*, Morehouse Publishing, 1999

Godfrey, John, 'The English Parish 600–1300', *Church History Outlines No. 3*, SPCK, 1969

Green, Michael, *Evangelism in the Early Church*, Kingsway, 2003

Guder, Darrell L., *Missional Church*, Eerdmans, 1998

Harper, Michael, *Let My People Grow*, Logos International, 1977

Harris, James F., *Philosophy at 33 1/3 rpm*, Open Court, 1993

Hendriksen, William, *Mark*, Banner of Truth Trust, 1975

Henry, Matthew, *Commentary on the Whole Bible, Matthew–John*, Macdonald Publishing Company

Hick, John, *Faith and Knowledge*, Fontana, 1974

Hollenweger, Walter J., 'Evangelism: A Non Colonial Model', *Journal of Pentecostal Theology* 7 (1995), pp. 107–128

Hunter, George, *How to Reach Secular People*, Abingdon, 1992

Jeremias, Joachim, *Jerusalem in the Time of Jesus*, Fortress Press, 1969

Kärkkäinen, Veli Matti, 'Towards a Theology and Ecclesiology of the Spirit', *Journal of Pentecostal Theology*, Issue 14 (1999)

Kreider, Eleanor, *Enter His Gates*, Marshall Pickering, 1989

Kümmel, W.G., *Introduction to the New Testament*, SCM Press, 1965

Kydd, Ronald A., *Charismatic Gifts in the Early Church*, Hendrickson Publishers, 1984

Leach, John, *Liturgy and Liberty*, MARC, 1989

Lightfoot, J.B., *Saint Paul's Epistle to the Galatians*, Macmillan & Company, 1921

Lloyd-Jones, D.M., *Christian Unity*, Banner of Truth Trust, 1980

Lyne, Peter, *First Apostles Last Apostles*, Sovereign World, 1999

MacMullen, Ramsay, *Christianizing the Roman Empire*, Yale University Press, 1984

Marshall, Tom, *Understanding Leadership*, Sovereign World, 1991

Miller, Donald E., *Reinventing American Protestantism*, University of California Press, 1999

Moo, Douglas J., *The Epistle to the Romans*, Eerdmans, 1996

Morgenthaler, Sally, *Worship Evangelism*, Zondervan, 1995

Morphew, Derek, *Breakthrough Discovering the Kingdom*, Vineyard International Publishing, 1991

Morris, Leon, *Ministers of God*, InterVarsity Press, 1973

Neuhaus, Richard John, *Freedom for Ministry*, Eerdmans, 1979

Newbiggin, Leslie, *Foolishness to the Greeks*, SPCK, 1986

——, *The Gospel in a Pluralistic Society*, SPCK, 1989

Newton, Flew R., *Jesus and His Church*, Caledonian International Book Manufacturing Ltd, 1998

Neyrey, Jerome H., *The Social World of Luke–Acts*, Hendrickson Publishers, 1991

Niebuhr, Richard, *Christ and Culture*, Harper & Row, 1951

Ogden, Greg, *The New Reformation*, Zondervan, 1990

Oswald, Roy M. and Otto Kroeger, *Personality Type and Religious Leadership*, The Alban Institute, 1996

Peck, Scott M., *The Different Drum*, Arrow Books, 1988

Penny, John, 'The Testing of New Testament Prophecy', *Journal of Pentecostal Theology* 10 (1997), pp. 35–84

Peters, George W., *A Theology of Church Growth*, Zondervan, 1981

Pitt-Watson, Ian, *A Primer for Preachers*, Baker, 1986

Radice, Betty (ed.), *The Cloud of Unknowing and Other Works*, Penguin, 1961

Richardson, Don, *Peace Child*, G/L Publications, 1974

Ridderbos, Herman, *Paul, an Outline of His Theology*, Eerdmans, 1975

Robinson, Thomas, *Studies in Romans*, Kregel Publications, 1982

Ruthven, Jon, *On the Cessation of the Charismata: The Protestant Polemic on Postbiblical Miracles*, Sheffield Academic Press, 1993

Ryle, John Charles, *Expository Thoughts on the Gospels, St Luke Vol. 1*, William Hunt & Company, 1884

Salter, Darius, *American Evangelism: Its Theory and Practice*, Baker, 1996

Schatzmann, Siegfried, *A Pauline Theology of Charismata*, Hendrickson Publishers, 1989

Schlatter, Adolf, *Romans: The Righteousness of God*, trans. Siegfried S. Schlatter, Hendrickson Publishers, 1995

Schwarz, Christian A., *Natural Church Development*, Church Smart Resources, 1996

Scott, Scott, *Like a House on Fire: Renewal in Postmodern Culture*, Cornerstone, 1997

Seligman, Martin E.P., 'Boomers', *Psychology Today*

Shaw, George Bernard, *Saint Joan*, Penguin Books, 1951

Sjogren, Steve, *Conspiracy of Kindness*, Vine Books, 1993

Snyder, Howard A., *The Community of the King*, InterVarsity Press, 1980

——, *New Wineskins*, Marshall, Morgan & Scott, 1975

Stedman, Ray C., *Bodylife*, Discovery House Publishers, 1972

Stevens, R. Paul, *The Abolition of the Laity*, Paternoster Press, 1999

Stevenson, J., *A New Eusebius*, SPCK, 1963

Stott, John R.W., *God's New Society: The Message of Ephesians*, InterVarsity Press, 1979

Strobel, Lee, *Inside the Mind of Unchurched Harry and Mary*, Zondervan, 1993

Stronstrad, Roger, *The Prophethood of All Believers*, Sheffield Academic Press, 1999

Sweet, Leonard, *Faithquake*, Abingdon, 1994

Synave, Paul and Pierre Benoit, *Prophecy and Inspiration. A*

Commentary on the Summa Theologica 11–11, Questions 171–178, Desclee Company, 1961

Thwaithes, James, *The Church Beyond the Congregation*, Paternoster Press, 1999

Tidball, Derek, *The Social Context of the New Testament*, Paternoster Press, 1983

Van Engen, Charles, *God's Missionary People*, Baker Book House, 1991

Vincent, Thomas, *The Shorter Catechism Explained from Scripture*, Banner of Truth Trust, 1980 (originally published 1674)

Wagner, C. Peter, *The New Apostolic Churches*, Regal, 1998

Walsh, Brian J., 'Derrida and the Messiah', *Regeneration Quarterly*, Spring 1999

Warfield, B.B., *Counterfeit Miracles*, Charles Scribner's Sons, 1918

Warren, Robert, *In the Crucible*, Highland Books, 1989

Watson, David, *I Believe in Evangelism*, Eerdmans, 1976

Williams, Colin, *Faith in a Secular Age*, Collins, 1966

Wilson, Geoffrey B., *Ephesians*, Banner of Truth Trust, 1978

Wimber, John, *Power Evangelism*, Hodder & Stoughton, 1985

Wright, Nigel, *Challenge to Change*, Kingsway, 1991

Wuthnow, Robert, *After Heaven: Spirituality in America Since the 1950s*, 1998